9355 113th St #8576,
Seminole, FL 33772
727-301-8204
RichterPublishing.com
admin@richterpublishing.com

Richter Publishing LLC has streamlined the writing and publishing process so anyone can become an author in only four weeks! With over 100 titles published and over 40 Amazon Best Sellers from all over the world, they're reinventing the publishing industry!

Forthcoming Titles

About **Richter Publishing**® LLC

Tara Richter is the President of Richter Publishing LLC. She specializes in helping business owners how to write their non-fiction story in 4 weeks & publish a book in order to become an expert in their industry. She has been featured on CNN, ABC, Daytime TV, FOX, SSN, Channel 10 News, USA TODAY, Beverly Hills Times and radio stations all over the world.

Her degree is in Graphic Design and she worked in the copy and print industry in the Silicon Valley. She has written and published 15 of her own books in just a few short years. Tara now has published many other authors all over the world including Anthony Amos & celebrity entrepreneur, Kevin Harrington, Shark from ABC's "Shark Tank" with their joint book, "How to Catch a Shark." She has also worked with many doctors, lawyers, non-profits and Fortune 500 Corporations such as Blooming Inc.

She started Richter Publishing in 2013 because authors kept coming to her asking how she did her own books. They were fed up with their publishers, so she asked what their struggles were and that's how she created the packages. To take away the pain points author were facing. To make it as easy as possible and help solve their problems as new authors. Now over 10 years in business there are many new amazing things learned after surviving a global pandemic and bad economic times. One thing she is, damn persistent. A zombie apocalypse will not take down this indie house!

Keep your head up and always look at the silver lining.

Tara Richter

A UFO Story

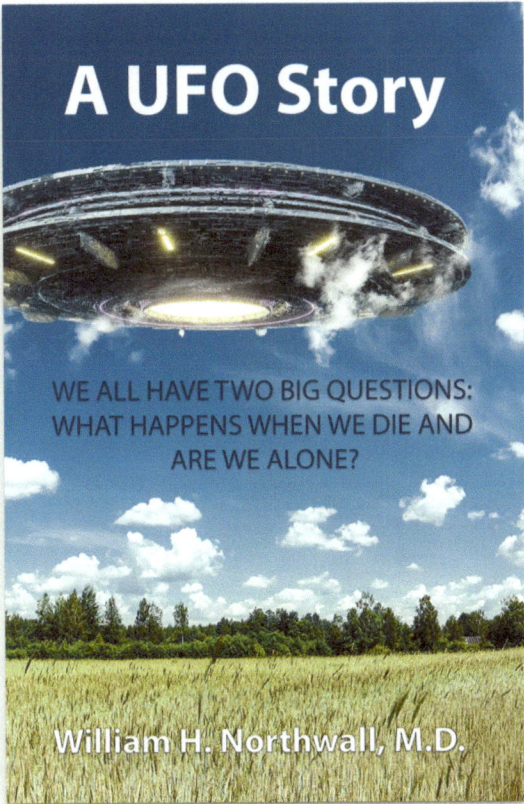

A UFO Story

By William H. Northwall M.D.

Polls tell us that the majority of Americans believe in UFOs. While government recently acknowledged the existence of UFOs, it is widely believed that government knows much more than they've released to the public. So where can someone curious about this subject go to find more specific information? I believe that a powerful alternative source of information can be found on the internet from witnesses, whistle-blowers, academic researchers, military experts, and scores of interested people, although separating fact from fiction may be difficult. My UFO book is an experiment and champions this alternative approach.

Published:November 14, 2022
Language: English
Paperback: 215 pages
ISBN-13: 979-8357349255
Item Weight : 10.9 ounces
Dimensions: 6 x 0.38 x 9 inches

Price: Paperback $23.00
Kindle: $5.99

This Cat is Photoshopped: The Book

By Tara Richter

A funny book for cat lovers by cat lovers. It puts your favorite feline in precarious situations. A cat mom or dad will volunteer a photo of their fur baby on a Facebook groups and let designers have a go at it. Sorry kitties, it's all their fault what happened to you. Some shops are bad, quick and all are super cheesy. So cheesy.

Price: $10.00
Published: November 19, 2022
Language: English
Paperback: 37 pages
ISBN-10: 1954094280
ISBN-13: 978-1954094284

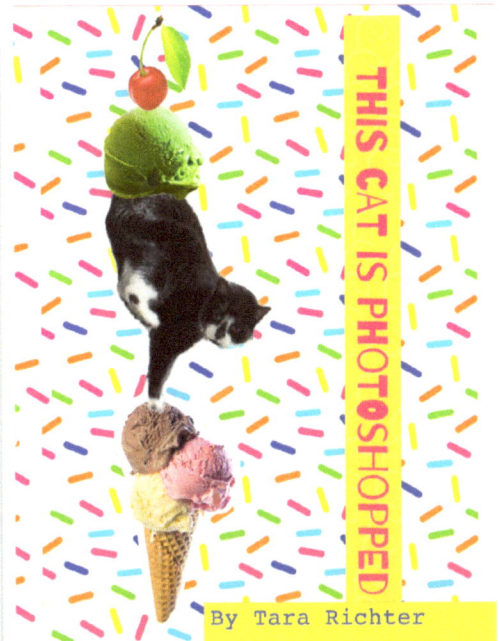

Mystery of the Vamours: New Beginnings

By Mercedes Hubert

Strange things have always happened around Anya Marie Harris — wind gusts that come from nowhere, bullies getting hurt even though she never touches them—but she can never explain these mysteries. Until, on her sixteenth birthday she and her adopted mom decide to look for her birth parents. Nothing can prepare her for the truth of who her family is, or the world she is about to be thrust into — a world of magic, mystical creatures, and demon werewolves. Can she learn to harness her gifts in time to protect herself from the monsters that have hunted her family her whole life? Can she accept who she was meantto be before her family pays the price? This coming-of-age story will take you on the adventure of a lifetime, as Anya is thrust into a world of danger, betrayal and monsters.

Published: March 1, 2022
Language: English
Paperback: 169 pages
ISBN-10: 1954094213
ISBN-13: 978-1954094215
Item Weight: 8.3 ounces
Dimensions : 6 x 0.39 x 9 inches

Price: Paperback $15.00
Hardback: $20.00
Kindle: $4.99

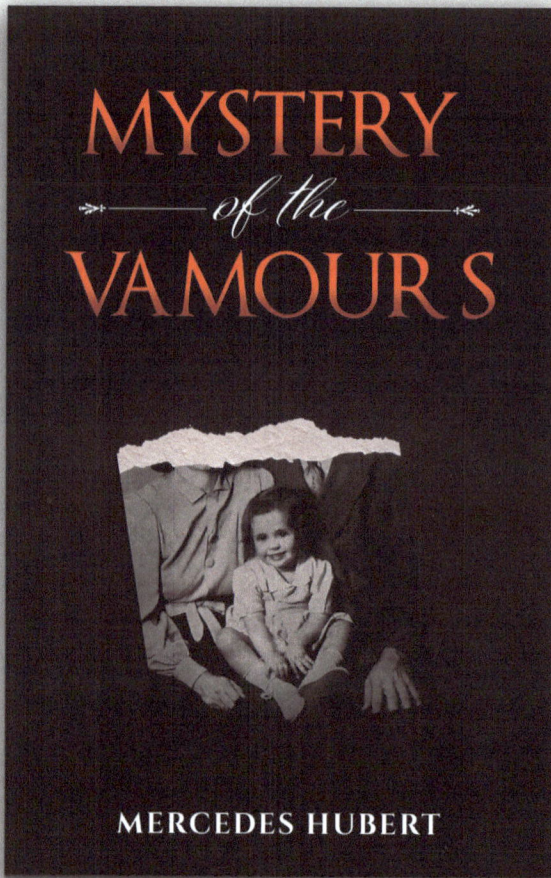

Creating Wealth, Investing Over a Lifetime

A GUIDE TO UNDERSTANDING THE STOCK MARKET

By William H. Northwall

This book is for young adults and older adults who have never had exposure to the stock market. My goal is to educate readers about the huge potential for accumulating a large amount of money in the stock market over time.

What you can learn withing these pages are:
-Stock market jargon
-Different ways to assess a stock's value
-Doing discounted cash flow analysis
-How to construct a stock portfolio
-Develop an investment plan
-Assemble a team of advisors to help you achieve financial security
-Clarifying your stock analysis through communicating with other investors
-Avoiding hazards to wealth creation

Published: April 18, 2022
Language: English
Paperback: 165 pages
ISBN-13: 979-8439714414
Item Weight : 10.9 ounces
Dimensions: 6 x 0.38 x 9 inches

Price: Paperback $15.00
Kindle: $4.99

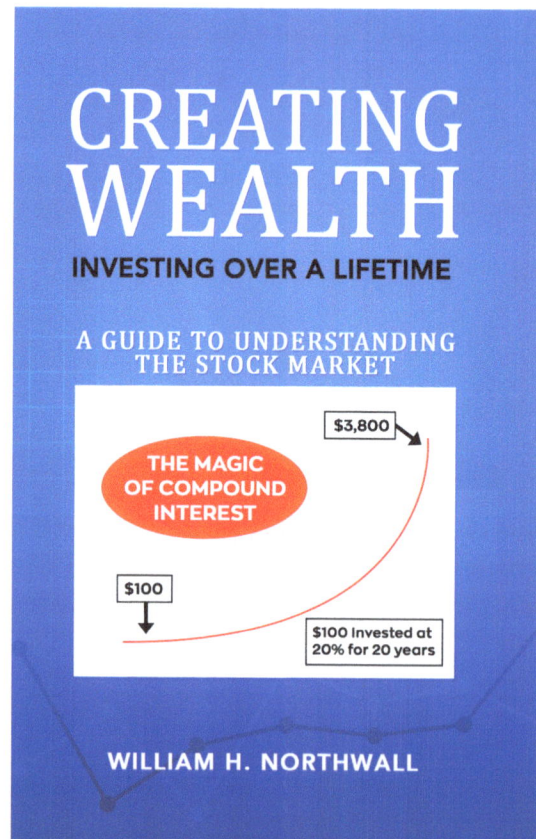

Seasons of Change

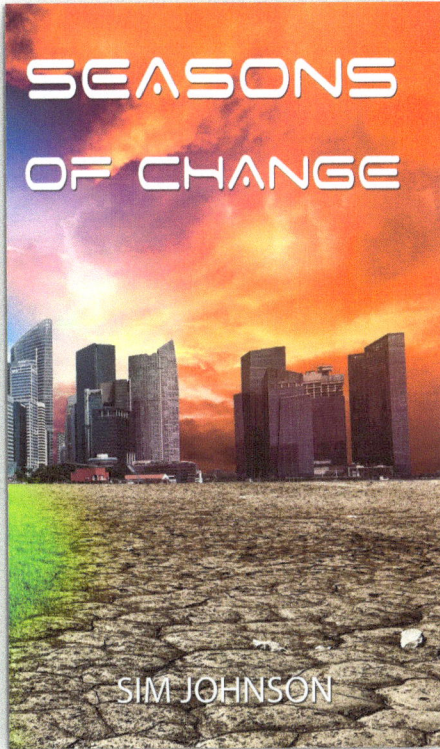

By Sim Johnson (Author) & Maurice Billington (Editor)

Nature has finally turned against man. Weather conditions are extreme and unbearable, forcing people everywhere to come to terms with their reckless disregard for the earth that we call home. That is until one courageous soul, Sarah Newman, begins a journey to change the fate of humankind and protect those that might otherwise perish from an upcoming apocalyptic freeze. How does an ordinary woman fare against the anger of nature and the force of the elements. Will she succeed where others have tried and failed? There's only one way to find out.

Publisher: April 12, 2022
Language: English
Paperback:100 pages
ISBN-10:1945812710
ISBN-13: 978-1945812712
Item Weight: 3.84 ounces
Dimensions:5 x 0.23 x 8 inches

Price: Paperback $15.00
Kindle: $5.99

Work & Live Anywhere: Island Hopping in Greece

By Tara Richter

Yes, you can travel the world and while you are working. The world has changed. If you are a digital nomad, or want to be, then this is the book for you! Or if you just want to travel and learn more about Greece and what it's like in a post Covid world. This has all the tips n' tricks to start globe trotting and get out there again. Check out my blog to keep up to date with new countries and book releases as well as retreats and fun stuff! www.nomadpublisher.com

Price: $30 in color - Paperback $20 - Kindle $2.99
Publisher: October 25, 2022
Language: English
Hardcover:145 pages
ISBN-10:1954094272
ISBN-13: 978-1954094277
Item Weight: 8.6 ounces
Dimensions: 5.5 x 0.53 x 8.5 inches

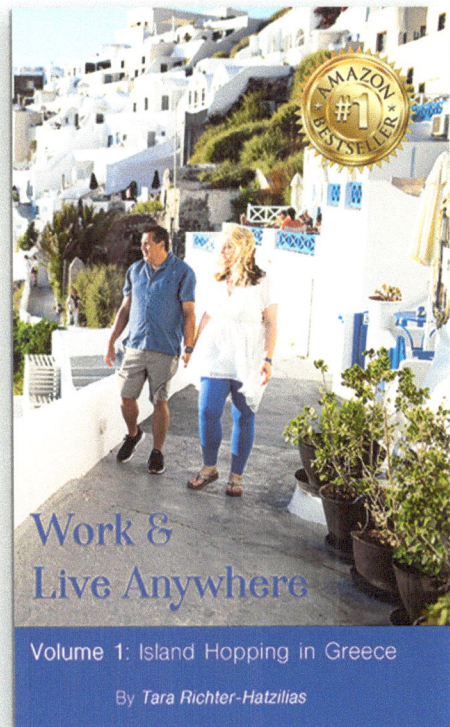

Freelance Writing: How to Make Money

By Peter Saxton Schroeder

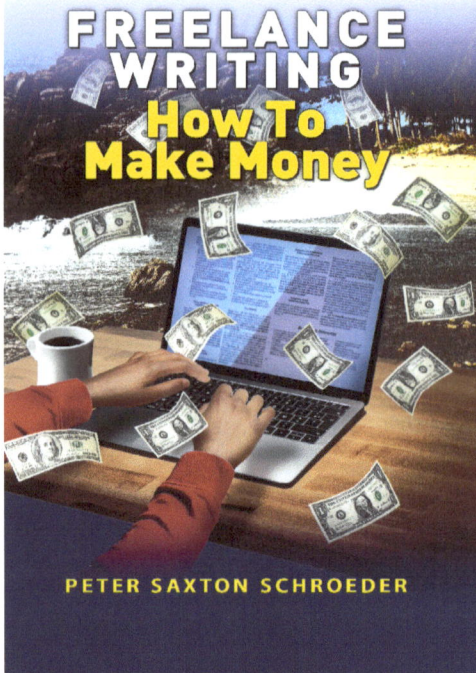

You can make BIG money with freelance writing.

Pursue your dream lifestyle and earn a great living too. Peter Schroeder, a 30-year freelance writer, debunks the myth so persuasive among other freelancers that poverty is the price to pay for doing the work they love. He presents tips and strategies that enable both beginning and established freelance writers to turn their craft into a highly profitable business.

Price: $15.00
Paperback: 145 pages
Published: November 10th 2021
Language: English

ISBN-10: 954094-11-6
ISBN-13: 978-1-954094-11-6
Dimensions 5 x 8 inches
Shipping Weight: 1.36 lbs

The Buffalo Scout

The Hero We Have Been Waiting For

by Stephen McDonald

As the US continues to settle the west in the wake of the civil war, one unlikely scout distinguishes himself as white settlers and freed slaves alike look to the US army for protection. The Buffalo Scout, a runaway slave himself, proves to be their best hope and craftiest warrior. With the skills it took to successfully deceive slave hunters, the tracking knowledge of several Indian tribes who harbored him on his journey west, and the support of the US army, no mission is too large for this vanguard. This work of historical fiction tells a story that has been left out of history, from a time when no one wanted to believe a black man could survive on his own, let alone fight legendary and heroic battles.

Price: $20.00
Paperback: 240 pages
Published: July 30, 2021
Language: English

ISBN-10: 1954094108
ISBN-13: 978-1954094109
Dimensions: 6 x 0.29 x 9 in
Shipping Weight: 6.4 oz

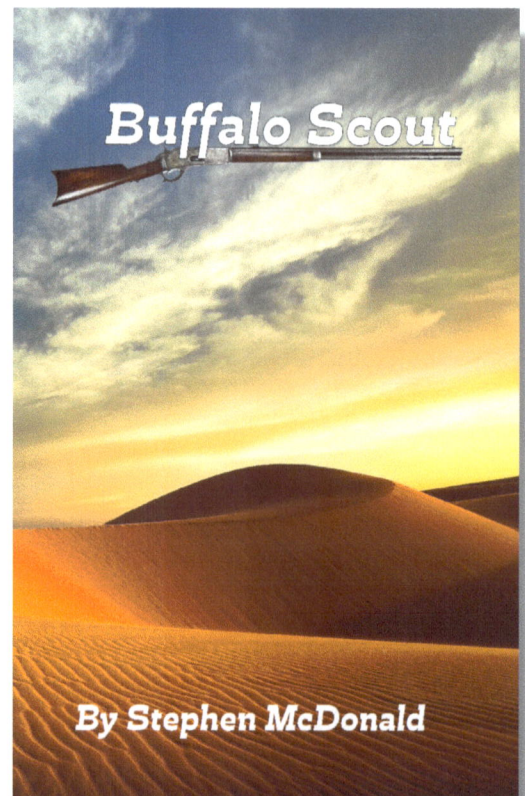

Dr. Marsha and the Case of the Missing Hot Dogs and Marshmallows

A 1-MD-POUCH Mystery

By Dr. Rachel Wellner M.D.

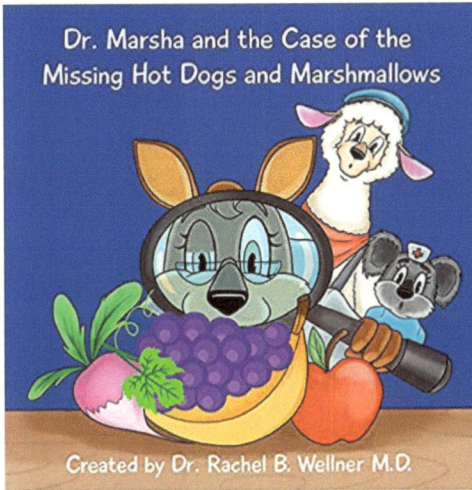

Dr. Marsha and her crew are living in Australia teaching healthy habits to the other animals in their town. But she turns into Doctoroo! to help solve mysteries all over the world! In this book, they fly to America to find out who stole all the marshmallows and hotdogs from the 4th of July cookout. Who could it be?!

Price: $16.00
Paperback: 47 pages
Published: June 1, 2021
Language: English

ISBN-10: 195409406X
ISBN-13:978-1954094062
Dimensions 8.5 x .12 x 8.5 in
Shipping Weight: 4.8 oz

Callie: The Crazy Callico

By Tara Richter

Callie might look like a sweet, innocent cat... but as soon as you let your guard down, her calico instincts kick in and she becomes Ninja Callie! The Adventures of Callie the Crazy Calico Cat, is a fun interactive book for children to teach them about pet adoption, feline leukemia and go into the mind-set of your favorite feline pet. This is a series of books that follows Callie on her daily adventures of living with her human family. Life with a calico cat is never a dull moment. This is the first book in the series that goes over the story of Callie as a kitten and being adopted from the shelter and her new life.

Price: $15.00
Paperback: 28 pages
Published: May 28, 2021
Language: English
oz

ISBN-10: 1954094043
ISBN-13: 978-1954094048
Dimensions: 8.5 x 0.07 x 8.5 in
Shipping Weight: 3.35

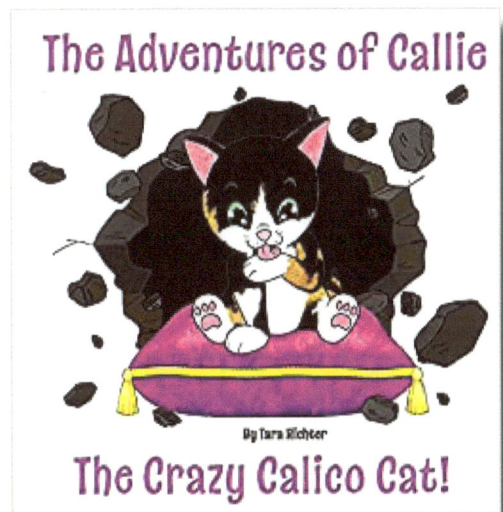

The Rock Shall Dance

By Peter Saxton Schroeder

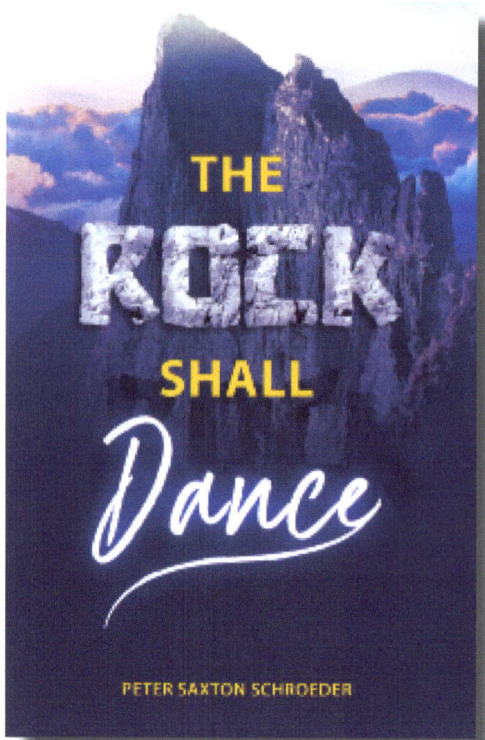

As readers of this autobiography soon discover, Peter Schroeder has lived out both traditional and divergent lifestyles. Armed with degrees from Princeton (B.S.E.), University of New Mexico (M.S.E.), and Stanford (M.B.A.), he carved out successful careers in nuclear weapons testing and international business. Interspersed with his professional endeavors, he had stints of hopping freight trains across the country, hitchhiking around Europe, slacking as a surfer dude, impersonating a priest, living in four countries, receiving not one but two presidential deferments from the Viet Nam draft, living in ashrams in India and Oregon, and battling a fatal form of bone marrow cancer. In current times he can be found skiing, sailing, scuba diving, or pursuing other adventures at hot spots around the globe as an outdoor travel writer. When he's not on the road, he and his wife Risa divide their time between homes in Seattle, Washington, and Sonoma, California, where they tend to their Syrah vineyard and boutique winery.

Price: $20.00
Paperback: 465 pages
Published: April 1, 2021
Language: English

ISBN-10: 1954094027
ISBN-13: 978-1954094024
Dimensions 6 x 1.05 x 9 in
Shipping Weight: 1.36 lbs

Call Out!
Learn to Love Yourself and Find Love

By Senada Cindy Nuredin

Life is hard, but love is harder. If you are still struggling with loving yourself or finding true love, then grab a bottle of wine, get this book and settle in for a wild ride that will change your life!

Price: $15.00
Paperback: 126 pages
Published: April 14, 2021
Language: English

ISBN-10: 1954094051
ISBN-13: 978-1954094055
Dimensions: 6 x 0.29 x 9 in
Shipping Weight: 6.4 oz

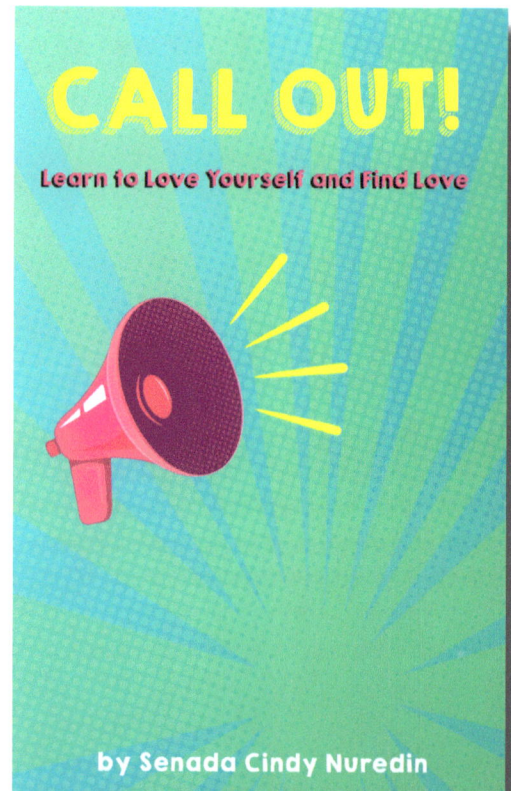

How to Run a Business During a Zombie Apocalypse

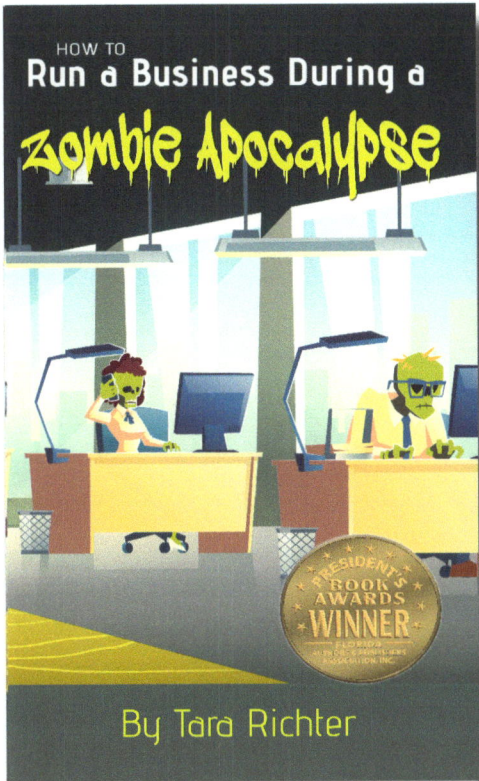

By Tara Richter

2020: the year of zombies, toilet paper shortages and murder hornets. Who would have thought we would live to see "The Walking Dead" come to life? Not me. We are living in a real life horror movie. And to top it off, some of us are trying to run a business during the most unprecedented times in our history. Where are our guidelines? Where is our leadership? Most of us are running around like chickens with our heads cut off because the sky really is falling. This book is full of real life tips on how we as entrepreneurs can keep our businesses afloat during a pandemic.

Price: $10.00
Paperback: 141 pages
Published: October 29, 2020
Language: English

ISBN-10: 1954094019
ISBN-13: 978-1954094017
Dimensions 5 x 0.32 x 8 in
Shipping Weight: 5.1 oz

For the Health of It
Over 350 Easy and Healthy Recipes

By Alexander Todrow

This book includes well over 350 recipes which were home-developed over the years "for the health of it". The book is about good nutrition and sensible diet. The recipes are simple and require short preparation and cooking times. Additionally, the recipes are flexible, many of which include provisions for substitution of individual food items specified. The foods to be used for preparation of the recipes are intended to be whole, unprocessed, and rich in nutrients. Some of the recipes included in this book meet the criteria of different diets, such as DASH, Ketogenic, Paleo, Vegetarian, Vegan, Mediterranean, etc.

Price: $45.00
Paperback: 320 pages
Published: October 9, 2020
Language: English

ISBN-10: 1945812982
ISBN-13: 978-1945812989
Dimensions: 8.5 x 0.76 x 11 in
Shipping Weight: 2.02 lb

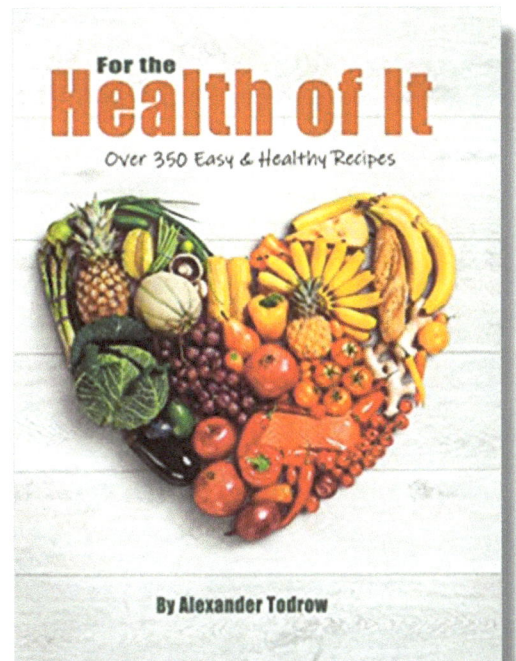

Riley & Milo

A Puppy's Story of Coping with Grief & Loss

By Cassie L D'Addeo LMFT

Processing death with a child is not an easy task. In fact, many people find it overwhelming and do not know how to initiate the conversation with young children. Using books, or bibliotherapy, as a method of explaining loss and grief is an effective tool for complex conversations. The book Riley and Milo leads young readers through the stages of grief such as: denial, anger, bargaining, sadness and acceptance. As the puppy Riley is processing the death of her best friend Milo, she explains her feelings and the impact of Milo's death on her life. This book was created to help naturalize the emotions and experiences of young readers who are coping with grief and loss.

Price: $15.00
Paperback: 41 pages
Published: April 6, 2021
Language: English

ISBN-10: 1954094035
ISBN-13: 978-1954094031
Dimensions 8.5 x 0.1 x 8.5 in
Shipping Weight: 4.3 oz

Also available in Spanish!

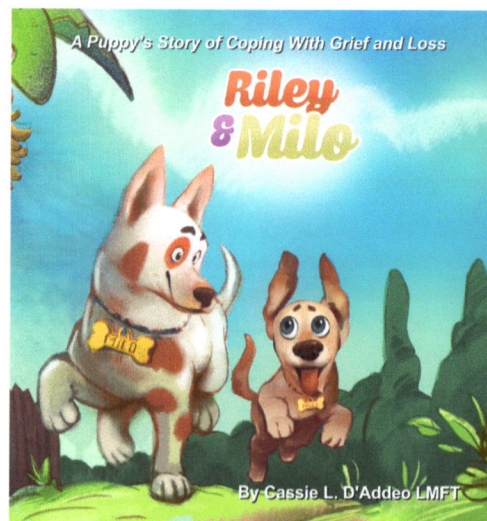

Doctoroo! & the Case of the Hacking Hippo

A 1-MD-POUCH Mystery

By Dr. Rachel Wellner M.D.

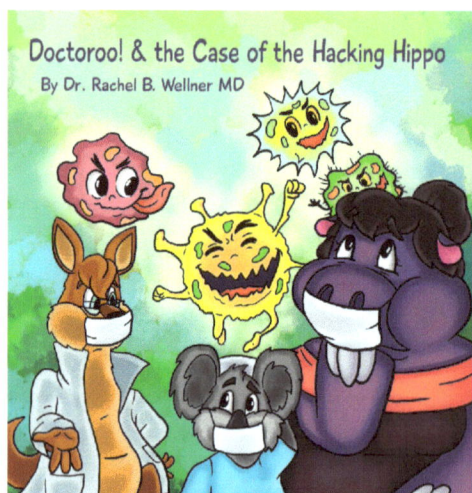

Dr. Marsha Roo and her crew are living in Australia teaching healthy habits to the other animals in their town. But she turns into Doctoroo! to help solve mysteries all over the world! In this book, Dr. Marsha and her friends help Hilda the Hippo, a famous Opera singer, find out why she is so sick. Will they solve the mystery and help Hilda get better before the Queen of England arrives to watch Hilda perform? Find out in this book along with germ fighting tips!

Price: $16.00
Paperback: 39 pages
Published: September 2, 2021
Language: English

ISBN-10: 1954094167
ISBN-13: 978-1954094161
Dimensions 8.5 x .12 x 8.5 in
Shipping Weight: 4.8 oz

Sold

By Ginger Rodeghero

The tables have turned on Christine in this daring sequel to Ginger Rodeghero's novel, "I'm Not For Sale." When she finds herself trapped in the clutches of her father's rival, Christine makes unlikely friends with Liam and Emma Walker. The hunter now becomes the hunted. But can they all make it out alive?

Price: $14.79
Paperback: 113 pages
Published: October 9, 2020
Language: English

ISBN-10: 1945812990
ISBN-13: 978-1945812996
Dimensions 5 x 0.26 x 8 in
Shipping Weight: 4.2 oz

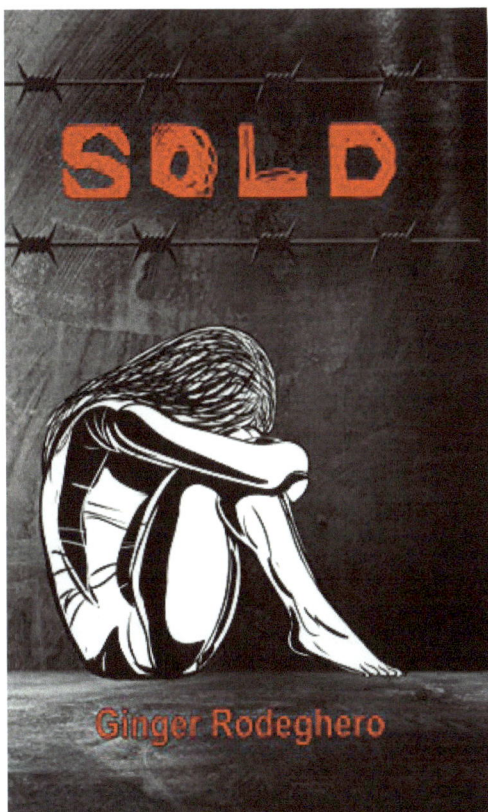

It's Hard to Die!
"Do I Hold On or Do I Let Go?"

By Enrique A. Cordero

Chapter one of this book is named, "So Here I Am—in a Place I Never Imagined." Don't find yourself there! Quite often, heart-wrenching, end-of-life decisions must be made in a moment's notice by laypersons and healthcare professionals alike. This book was written to help you understand many of the issues you may face, and help you unravel their complexity—so, when the time comes, you can think clearly and make informed decisions on behalf of the dying—be it you, loved ones, or your patients.

Price: $14.95
Paperback: 227 pages
Published: July 15, 2020
Language: English and Spanish

ISBN-10: 1702738116
ISBN-13: 978-1702738118
Dimensions 5 x 0.51 x 8 in
Shipping Weight: 11 oz

It's Hard to Die!
"Do I Hold On or Do I Let Go?"

Catastrophic illnesses can raise many end-of-life issues such as: Will my last wishes before I die be followed? What do I need to consider in my end-of-life planning? Will my decisions prolong life or prolong the dying process? ...and more.

Valuable information for healthcare personnel and laypersons.

Enrique A. Cordero

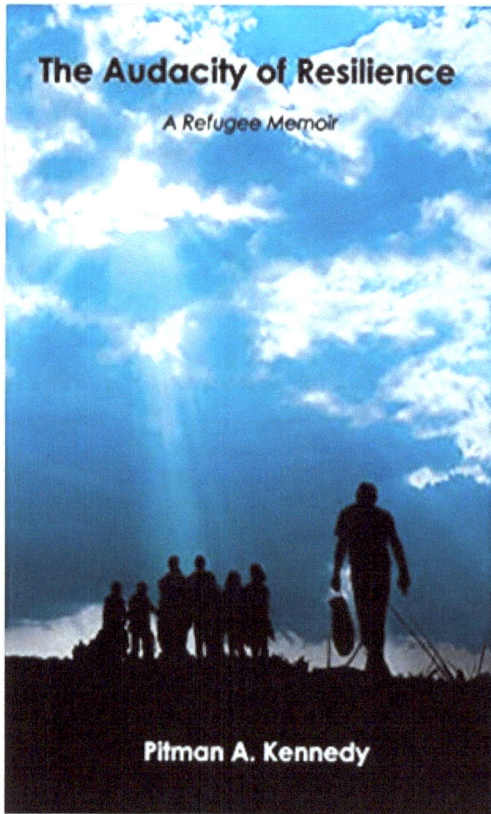

The Audacity of Resilience
A Refugee Memoir

By Pitman A. Kennedy

An inspirational memoir of a man who escaped war torn Liberia to eventually find asylum in America. However, it was not an easy road to travel. As a child, it took Pitman and his family almost two months to walk on foot from their country into Sierra Leone. With nothing but the clothes on their backs, they had to hide from rebels who were on a rampage amputating and murdering anyone who they thought were connected to the government. In his debut book, Kennedy takes you along his journey of being a refugee from a 3rd world country to becoming a successful businessman in the states. Find out more about Pitman on his website: www.sweatequityleadership.com.

Price: $15.00
Paperback: 106 pages
Published: June 11, 2020
Language: English

ISBN-10: 194581294X
ISBN-13: 978-1945812941
Dimensions 5 x 0.2 x 8 in
Shipping Weight: 6.1 oz

Women Who Want More
How to Create A Balanced and Fulfilled Life

By Dr. Rana Al-Falaki

Are you juggling to find balance in your life? Imagine how you'd feel if your life was just as you wanted it to be. If you could ask for what you wanted, create it and find the time to enjoy it. If you could change the thought of "I can't" to "I totally CAN!" Discover the answers in this powerful book: Discover what you truly want, How to set and maintain healthy boundaries, How to change the feeling of 'should' to want', Instant strategies to combine fun with the never-ending 'to-do' list, FREE guided meditations and additional downloadable resources including finding your purpose, how to deal with parents, partners and children, being healthy, creating abundance and having fun.

Price: $15.00
Paperback: 214 pages
Published: January 6, 2020
Language: English

ISBN-10: 1945812915
ISBN-13: 978-1945812910
Dimensions: 6 x 0.5 x 9 in
Shipping Weight:13.6 oz

Gasparilla
A Pirate's Tale

By Lisa Ballard

José Gaspar never intends to become a pirate, but after being falsely accused of stealing the crown jewels, it becomes his fate while trying to escape on a ship bound from Spain to Florida. After saving his best friend and freeing the crew from the ship's evil captain, he defeats the infamous Pierre LaFitte then claims the west coast of Florida as his pirate domain... until the Americans find him.

Price: $15.00
Paperback: 52 pages
Published: January 3, 2019
Language: English

ISBN-10: 1945812672
ISBN-13: 978-1945812675
Dimensions 6 x 0.1 x 9 in
Shipping Weight: 0.6 oz

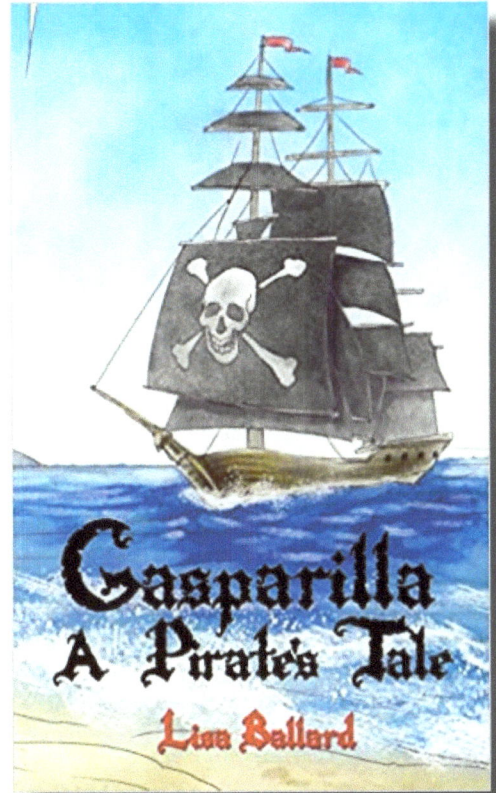

The Dating Jungle
Adult Coloring Book

By Tara Richter

This hilarious adult coloring book is the fourth in the Dating Jungle series. The author, Tara Richter, gives real-world dating advice to help you navigate the territory of popular dating apps like Tinder. Each very helpful tip has a corresponding therapeutic coloring page to help you de-stress from annoying dates. So pour yourself a glass of wine, get your colored pencils out, and have some fun! Post your finished pictures on social media with the hashtag #datingjunglecoloringbook and share with others in the jungle.

Price: $9.99
Paperback: 47 pages
Published: January 28, 2020
Language: English

ISBN-10: 1945812737
ISBN-13: 978-1945812736
Dimensions 8.5 x 0.1 x 11 in
Shipping Weight: 6.2 oz

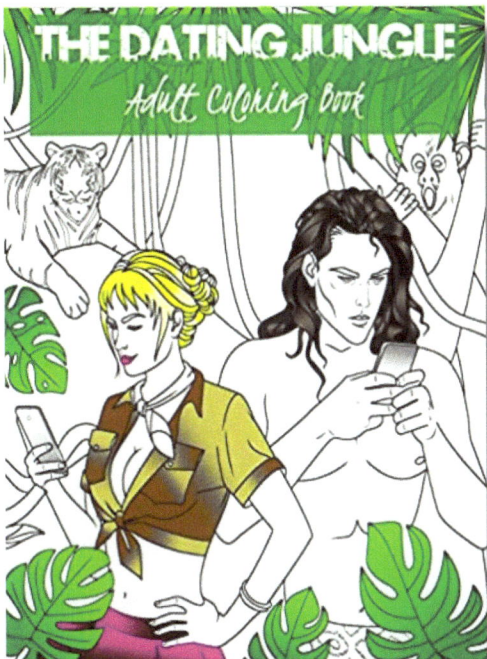

Life Is Golden

By Shea Miller

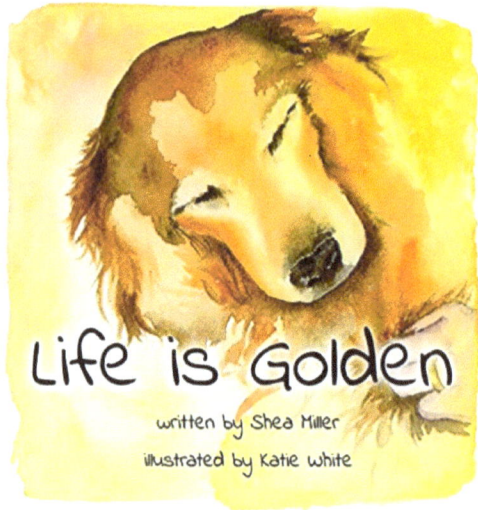

"Life is Golden" is about Chloe, a golden retriever that found herself in a rescue organization after being given up twice. This made Chloe feel sad and unwanted, and her fur coat was thin and dull. One day she met the Millers, her new forever family. As Chloe got used to her new Golden Life, she began to feel loved and part of a family. Because of this, her fur coat began to grow and grow and become full and shiny. Chloe felt like a lucky dog to be in this family, but it was the Millers who were the lucky ones and happy to have her in their lives.

Price: $15.00
Paperback: 28 pages
Published: February 1, 2019
Language: English

ISBN-10: 1945812729
ISBN-13: 978-1945812729
Dimensions 8.5 x 0.1 x 8.5 in
Shipping Weight: 3.7 oz

Scars of a Soldier

By Jonathan Bonnet

"Scars of a Soldier" follows Jonathan on his journey from a teenage delinquent to a soldier in Afghanistan. Jonathan shares his experiences growing up with a rocky childhood. He exposes the raw truth of dealing with depression, suicide and drugs. Climb into his mind and get a firsthand view of what it's like to go through the highs and lows to live a normal life and persevere.

Price: $22.00
Paperback: 398 pages
Published: April 15, 2019
Language: English

ISBN-10: 1945812761
ISBN-13: 978-1945812767
Dimensions: 6 x 0.9 x 9 in
Shipping Weight:1.5 lbs

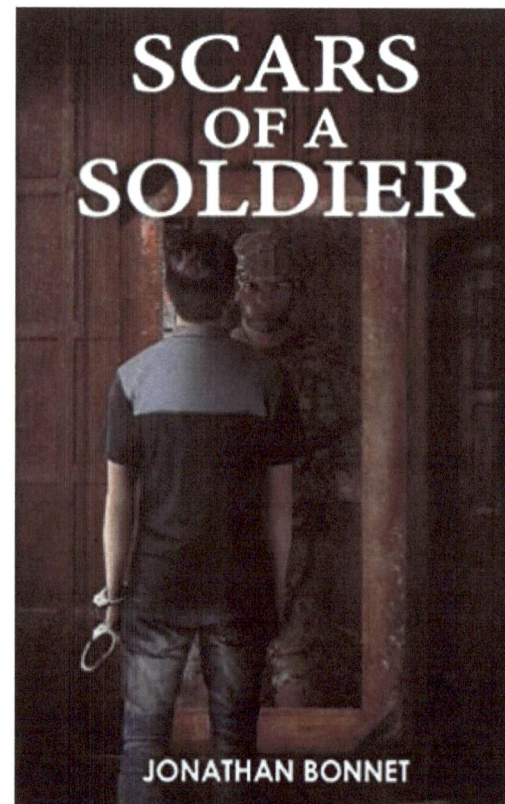

Ask Dr. Flo: 150 Tips
from Head to Toe for Less Pain & Better Function

By Dr. Florence Barber-Hancock

Sometimes it is little things in our daily lives that contribute to aches, pains, or the loss of functions that we have taken for granted. Does it hurt to walk up stairs or drive a long distance? Has carrying groceries or a briefcase become difficult? Can't sit at your computer without an achy neck? These short tips are arranged to help you quickly consider some common sources of discomfort. These gems of practical information offer readers a wealth of ideas that are easy to implement—with little or no cost—at home, at work, and in leisure activities.

Price: $15.00
Paperback: 142 pages
Published: June 29, 2019
Language: English

ISBN-10: 1945812788
ISBN-13: 978-1945812781
Dimensions 5.5 x 0.3 x 8.5 in
Shipping Weight: 8.5 oz

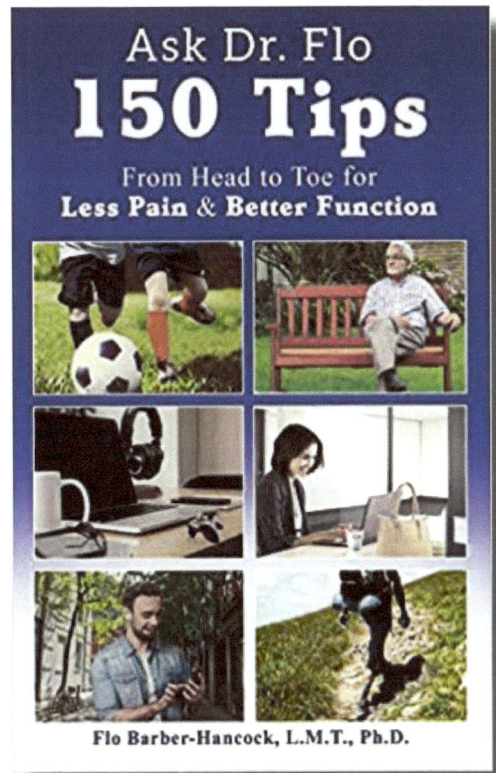

¡Spanish for You!
Spanish Course for Beginners and Advanced Students A1-B1

By Heidi McPherson

This Spanish course is a detailed guide to learning the Spanish language. Particularly, it is intended to help students approach real-language usage. In many lecciones, everyday topics are discussed, including very useful vocabulary.

Price: $35.00
Paperback: 419 pages
Published: September 18, 2019
Language: English

ISBN-10: 1945812796
ISBN-13: 978-1945812798
Dimensions 8.5 x 0.1 x 11 in
Shipping Weight: 2.6 lbs

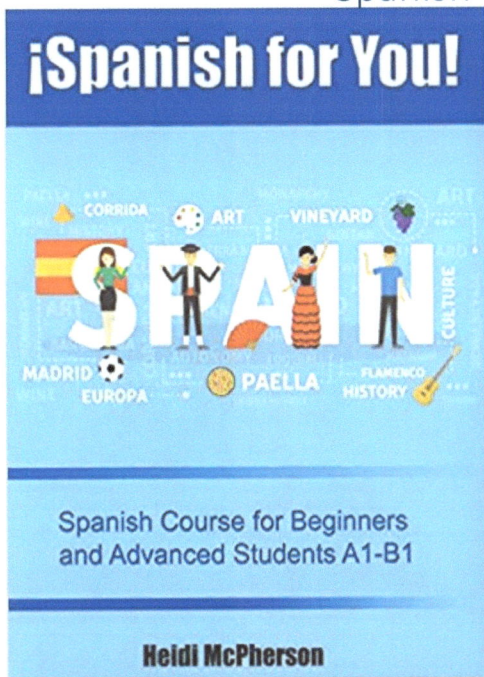

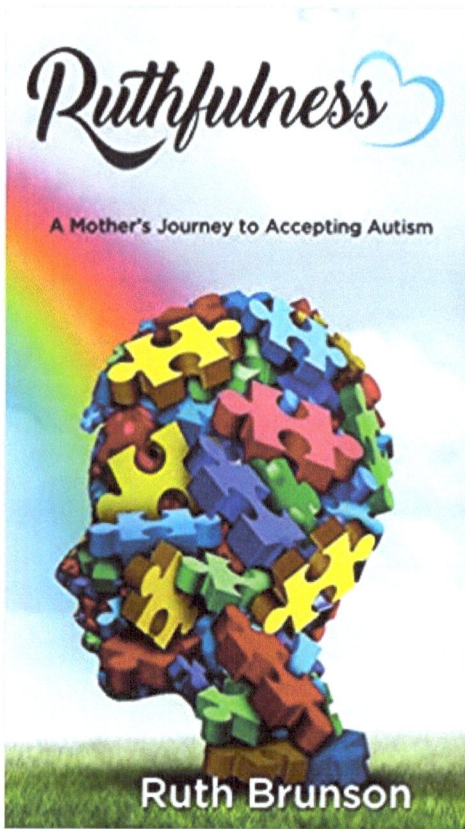

Ruthfulness
A Mother's Journey to Accepting Autism

By Ruth Brunson

A heart wrenching story of what it is really like to raise a child with Autism. Ruth leads us through the day to day struggles of early intervention that many families deal with in this era of children on the spectrum. It gives any family hope and laughter, that they too can overcome this disorder. Find out more on her website: www.ruthfulness.com

Price: $15.00
Paperback: 188 pages
Publishd: September 24, 2019
Language: English

ISBN-10: 1945812745
ISBN-13: 978-1945812743
Dimensions 5 x 0.4 x 8 in
Shipping Weight: 7 oz

Down to the Sea for Kicks

By Samuel Fullerton

Come aboard the S.S. Nectar and sail back to the 1960's in this memoir by Samuel Fullerton. A comical mix between "The Love Boat" and "Titanic," it unveils the real shenanigans that go on between musicians who work on the ship. No subject is taboo as the male group entertains the ship's passengers, while slipping through the tight grip of management to make for an epic adventure. Put on your sunscreen, grab a drink and cruise away with us.

Price: $20.00
Paperback: 325 pages
Published: September 27, 2019
Language: English

ISBN-10: 1945812818
ISBN-13: 978-1945812811
Dimensions 6 x 0.7 x 9 in
Shipping Weight:15.5 oz

I'm Not for Sale

By Ginger Rodeghero

When Shelby loses contact with her twin sister Sydney after a college party, she has no idea how dark the next few days will become. Their twin sense has always gotten them through anything, but Shelby can no longer sense her sister's energy. She knows something horrible has happened and will not stop until she finds her. But first Shelby has to risk her own safety by being entangled within an underground trafficking ring.

Price: $15.00
Paperback: 147 pages
Published: October 2, 2019
Language: English

ISBN-10: 194581280X
ISBN-13: 978-1945812804
Dimensions 5 x 0.3 x 8 in
Shipping Weight: 5.6 oz

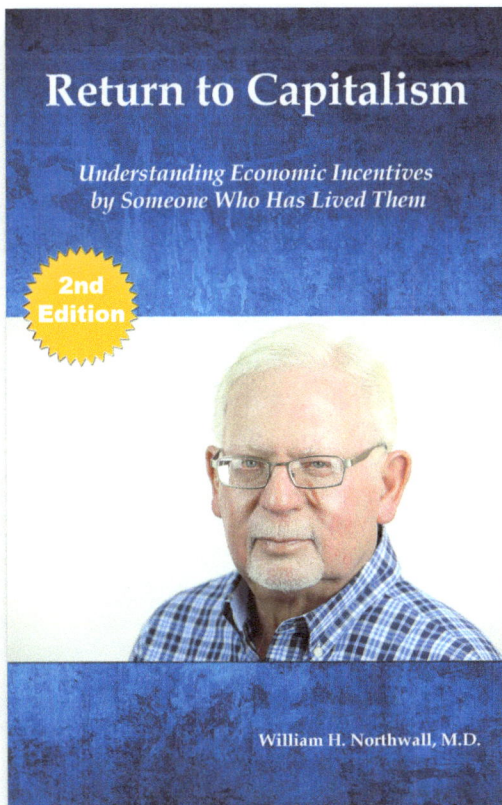

Return to Capitalism

Understanding Economic Incentives by Someone Who Has Lived Them

By William H. Northwall M.D.

My book is about the future, and the readers I wish to attract are the younger generations, especially those people attracted to liberal, progressive and socialistic ideals. The young tend to reject capitalism because anti-capitalism is all they've been taught. Thus, they believe that business is in the business of making money and not helping the poor or the environment. They have established views on the horrors of greed. Today, we are mired in a mess that our politicians of both parties have created; unbelievable public debt, excessive taxation stifling our economy, entitlements well on their way to insolvency, poor inner-city schools, unaffordable higher education, and the list goes on and on. The solution to most of our problems is a return of capitalistic approaches.

Published: JUNE 30, 2017
Language: English
Paperback: 288 pages
ISBN-13: 978-1546426523
Item Weight : 10.9 ounces
Dimensions: 5.5x.65x8.5 inches

Price: Paperback $20.00
Kindle: $9.99

Things They Fail to Tell You During Pregnancy
A Quick Guide and Insight

By Ashley Shayne Pierce

Ashley Shayne Pierce offers a detailed account of her own experiences as well as the important factors that often go untold with motherhood. Pierce explores every aspect of becoming a new parent, from contemplating pregnancy to advanced postpartum. She offers a myriad of suggestions, advice, and possible plans to follow when expecting, alongside honest encouragement, personal tips, and essential must-haves to aid during the sometimes-overwhelming journey.

Price: $15.00
Paperback: 118 pages
Published: January 27, 2018
Language: English

ISBN-10: 1945812311
ISBN-13: 978-1945812316
Dimensions 5.5 x 0.3 x 8.5 in
Shipping Weight: 7.4 oz

Prevail
Celebrate the Journey

By Alder Allensworth

After being diagnosed with a rare, usually fatal cancer, Alder Allensworth made a miraculous recovery and took on a sailing journey most would only dream of. Having lost one eye to cancer, Alder dedicated herself to a 1,200-mile trip to raise money and awareness for sailors with disabilities, and quickly realized that sailing the 12-foot Prevail from Florida to Maine presented a whole new set of challenges that she had never encountered before, even on the water. Prevail: Celebrate the Journey follows Alder's story from her diagnosis through her sailing expedition, and finally to the creation of a nonprofit sailing organization that provides instruction and recreation to people of all ages and abilities, Sailability Greater Tampa Bay.

Price: $20.00
Paperback: 190 pages
Published: February 3, 2018
Language: English

ISBN-10: 194581232X
ISBN-13: 978-1945812323
Dimensions 6 x 0.4 x 9 in
Shipping Weight:12.2 oz

Culture in 4D

The Blueprint for a Culture of Engagement, Ownership, and Bottom-Line Performance

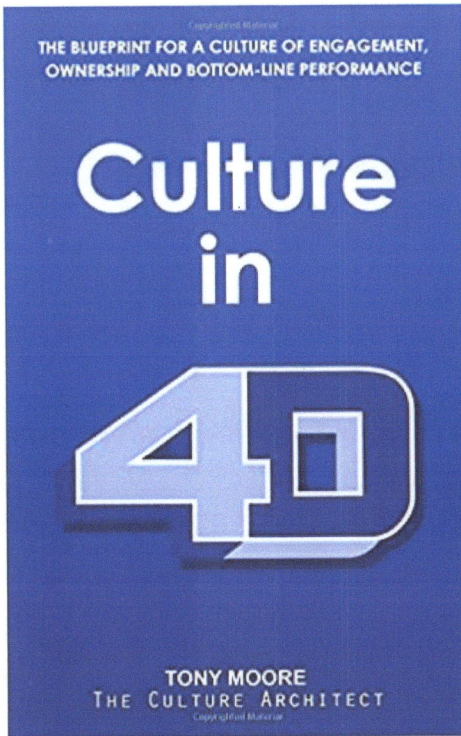

By Tony Moore

In simple, easy to follow language, "Culture in 4D" pulls the curtain back on the mystery behind the design and development of a strong team culture. Combining research, real-life stories, and solutions born out of experience, the Culture Architect, Tony Moore, provides leaders with the blueprint for embedding values and setting expectations, resulting in clearly defined Rules of Engagement. Much like he does in his presentations, Tony transforms abstract concepts into concrete, tangible, actionable steps. "Culture in 4D" empowers readers to take control of the work experience by engaging employees in a process where they Dream, Design, Develop, and Defend the desired culture.

Price: $15.00
Paperback: 130 pages
Published: February 19, 2018
Language: English

ISBN-10: 1945812192
ISBN-13: 978-1945812194
Dimensions 5.5 x 0.3 x 8.5 in
Shipping Weight: 7.8 oz

Striking Eight Bells

A Vietnam Memoir

By George Trowbridge

In Striking Eight Bells, George Trowbridge recounts his journey from the Midwest to a warship in the Gulf of Tonkin during the closing months of the Vietnam War. Choosing to enlist in the Navy at 19, versus being drafted into the military, Trowbridge left a wife and newborn son in the States as he traversed the oceans of the globe to fight in America's most unpopular war. George shares the details on life on board a naval destroyer during this era. This emotional story is not only historically focused, but it also is informative about life in the military, all filtered through the personal lens of a firsthand perspective.

Price: $22.00
Paperback: 308 pages
Published: February 21, 2018
Language: English

ISBN-10: 9781945812330
ISBN-13: 978-1945812330
Dimensions 6 x 0.7 x 9 in
Shipping Weight: 1.2 oz

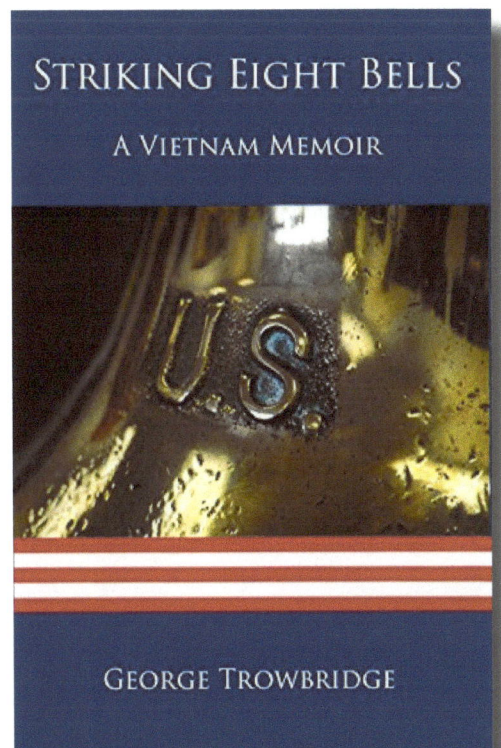

Proper Care and Feeding of a Huntin' Buddy
(Humor, with a Little Huntin' Thrown In)

By Bob Baldwin, Jay Ledbetter

No animals have been harmed in the making of this book.
Bob and Jay began their joint hunting experiences when Jay, the owner of Buffalo Mountain Ranch in Texas, reached out to Bob, owner of BowhuntingInfo.com from Michigan for help with a rogue bison bull on his ranch. Bob was able to help with a crazy hunter willing to get close enough to shoot that bull with a stick and a string. After that auspicious meeting, Bob and Jay hit it right off. Jay and Bob have written over 27 short stories about some of their escapades. These encompass trips into the wilds of northern Canada, the great Rocky Mountains, and into the cactus strewn land of Texas.

Price: $15.00
Paperback: 106 pages
Published: May 8, 2018
Language: English

ISBN-10: 1945812397
ISBN-13: 978-1945812392
Dimensions 5.5 x 0.2 x 8.5 in
Shipping Weight: 6.7 oz

Rhino
The Bully

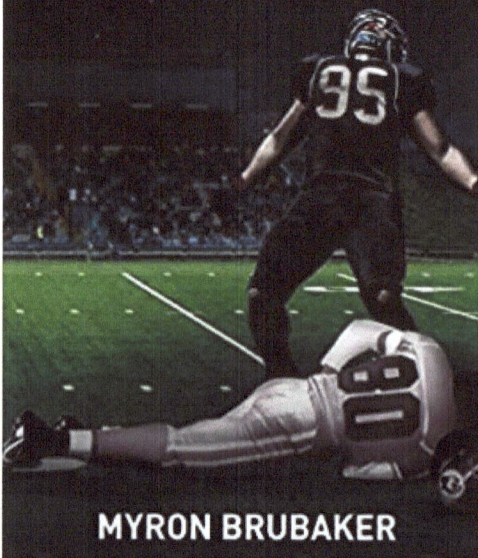

By Myron Brubaker

An inspirational novel about a bully redeemed
Henry Fitzwater is a troubled teen. He struggles to overcome the guilt of accidentally killing his parents in a house fire when he was a child. When Andy Reinhart befriends him, Andy gets in more trouble with his parents than he's ever been in. But by befriending Fitz, Andy helps him transform from a boy fighting everyone to a young man who can fight for others. Now, the school bully might be the only one who can save Andy. And, he'll have to use words instead of fists.

Price: $20.00
Paperback: 276 pages
Published: May 13, 2018
Language: English

ISBN-10: 1945812389
ISBN-13: 978-1945812385
Dimensions 5.5 x 0.6 x 8.5 in
Shipping Weight:14.9 oz

Work Sucks!
A Funny View of a Serious Problem

By Spencer Borisoff

"Work Sucks!" slaps the biggest, baddest, crudest, rudest bully the world has ever seen square on its jaw. Borisoff unleashes his unconventional take on conventional work topics like rush hour, bosses, the Sunday night shakes, performance reviews, alarm clocks, meaningless meetings, firings, and lightning-quick weekends. Borisoff's tongue is fresh but his unique voice shouts and shares a universal message: Work Sucks!

Price: $15.00
Paperback: 162 pages
Published: June 29, 2018
Language: English

ISBN-10: 1945812427
ISBN-13: 978-1945812422
Dimensions 6 x 0.4 x 9 in
Shipping Weight: 10.7 oz

Three Friends Limeade
Friends and Business Mix Together

By Brittney Kempink

A vividly illustrated children's book geared toward ages of 6-10 years old. Mrs. Kempink teaches entrepreneurial skills through the colorful characters in this book. Children open competing limeade stands and figure out how they can make money and work together. Includes a fun recipe to make and enjoy limeade at home with your family.

Price: $15.00
Paperback: 28 pages
Published: August 1, 2018
Language: English

ISBN-10: 1945812451
ISBN-13: 978-1945812453
Dimensions 8.5 x 0.1 x 11 in
Shipping Weight: 4.3 oz

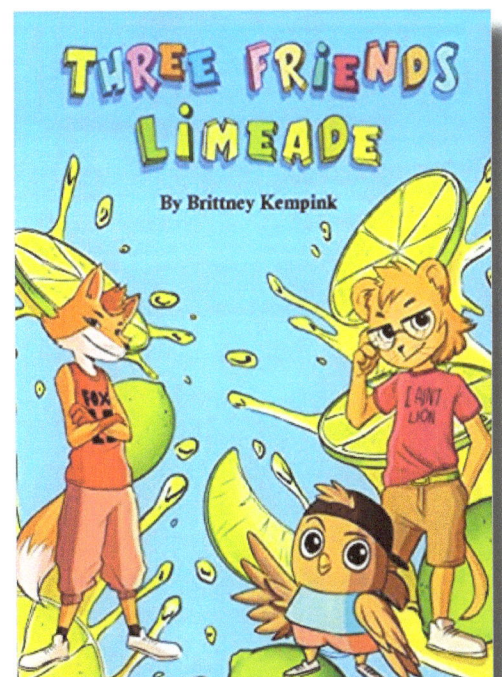

Millenial Marriages
A Military Relationship

By Jarron Webster

When young military couples are faced with the prospect of separation, sometimes they jump into a marriage to avoid the pain of being apart. In "Millennial Marriages: A Military Relationship," Jarron Webster explores the ins and outs of Mark and Wendy's journey through their first years after "I do." This means relocation as Mark is sent to multiple new bases for his job in the military, decisions about family planning, finances, and learning how to maintain trust when things get rocky. Can the couple stay true to themselves, and to each other, as they navigate the obstacle course that is a military marriage?

Price: $15.00
Paperback: 124 pages
Published: September 21, 2018
Language: English

ISBN-10: 1945812435
ISBN-13: 978-1945812439
Dimensions 5.5 x 0.3 x 8.5 in
Shipping Weight: 7.7 oz

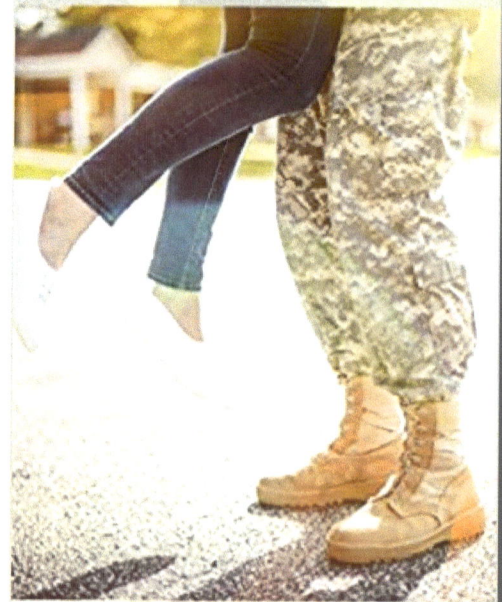

MILLENNIAL MARRIAGES
A MILITARY RELATIONSHIP

BY JARRON WEBSTER, M.B.A.
"THE TAMPA BOW TIE GUY"

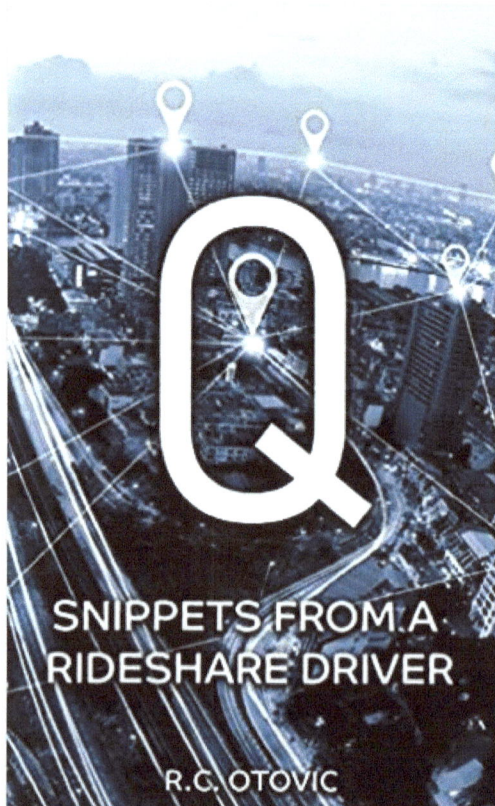

Q

SNIPPETS FROM A
RIDESHARE DRIVER

R.C. OTOVIC

Snippets from a Rideshare Driver

By R. C. Otovic

When C.D. Howell left his job in the spring of 2017 to become a full-time rideshare driver, he never imagined how easy it would be for passengers to open up and immerse him in their most private, intimate stories. Grab a coffee, light up a smoke, and sit back while he takes you on a journey through his customers' troubled daily lives. Ridesharing is a cultural phenomenon sweeping across the globe. This is the other side of rideshare travel—the side you never thought existed.

Price: $20.00
Paperback: 206 pages
Published: October 7, 2018
Language: English

ISBN-10: 1945812524
ISBN-13: 978-1945812521
Dimensions 6 x 0.5 x 9 in
Shipping Weight:13.1 oz

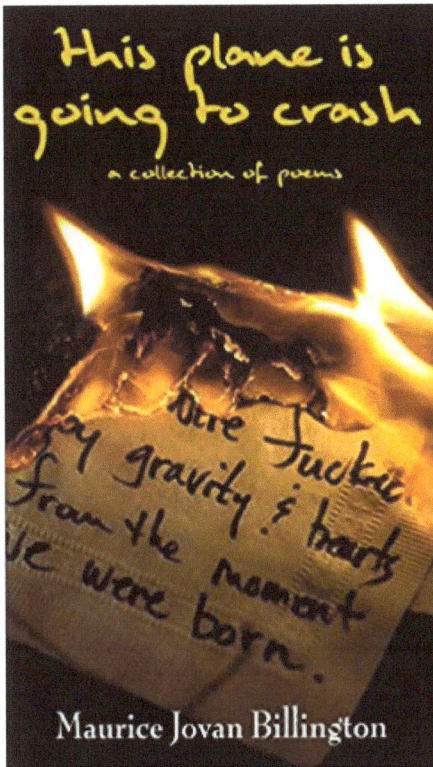

This Plane is Going to Crash

By Maurice Jovan Billington

A collection of poems about the debris left in the wake of love and desire.

Price: $15.99
Paperback: 144 pages
Published: October 8, 2018
Language: English

ISBN-10: 1945812567
ISBN-13: 978-1945812569
Dimensions 5 x 0.3 x 8 in
Shipping Weight: 7.5 oz

I Found Me

By Corey Hall

An inspirational story that brings light to an invisible enemy that millions of people suffer from in America, but don't want to talk about, Bipolar Disorder. In his debut memoir, "I Found Me," Corey Hall shares his experiences growing up with a mental illness he didn't know he suffered from until his twenties. He exposes the raw truth of dealing with depression, suicide and insomnia. Climb into his mind and get a firsthand view of what it's like to go through the highs and lows and how to live a normal life. Follow Corey on Instagram to keep up with his story @TruChef8384

Price: $15.00
Paperback: 102 pages
Published: October 23, 2018
Language: English

ISBN-10: 1945812559
ISBN-13: 978-1945812552
Dimensions 5.5 x 0.2 x 8.5 in
Shipping Weight: 6.6 oz

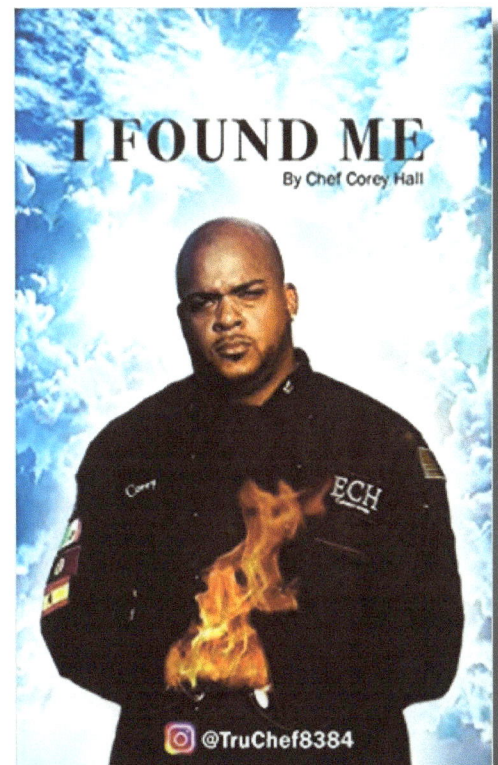

Brothers in War

By Ginger Rodeghero

Eric is a talented soccer player going into his Senior year of High School. He has hopes of landing a scholarship to play at the esteemed Syracuse University. Everything seems to be in alignment for the young athlete until his perfect world gets flipped upside down, when his sister is murdered by the Taliban in Afghanistan. Eric's life goes into a downward tail spin and he takes out his anger on the new student at school, Rasheed. The foreign exchange student is a brilliant soccer player and now Eric's scholarship is in jeopardy. But Rasheed has his own inner demons to deal with that could mess up his opportunities in America. Can these two boys put their cultural differences aside and help one another survive? Find out in this debut novel by Ginger Rodeghero.

Price: $15.00
Paperback: 202 pages
Published: November 20, 2018
Language: English

ISBN-10: 0960008101
ISBN-13: 978-0960008100
Dimensions 5 x 0.5 x 8 in
Shipping Weight: 9.9 oz

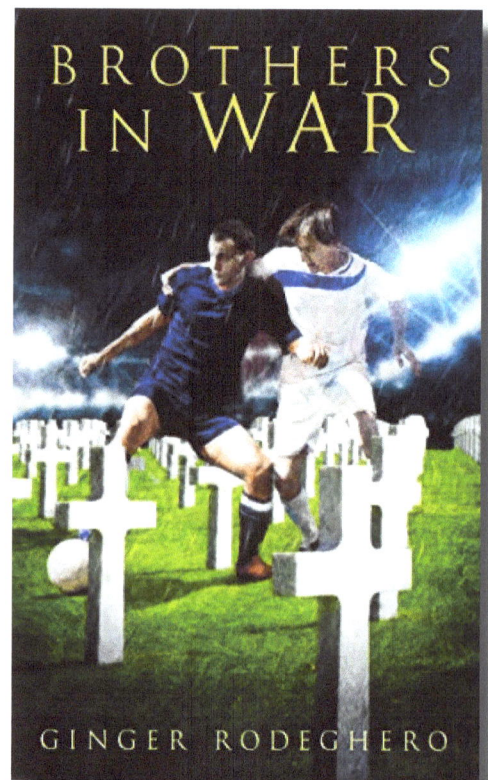

Gasparilla
Coloring and Activity Book

By Nastassia Clarke

Gasparilla was a Spanish nobleman until the day he fell in love with the sea. He hopped aboard a ship and gathered all of his closest friends to join his pirate crew. As he sailed around the world, he used treasure maps to find buried riches. He found chests filled with gold coins, glittering beads, and colorful jewels. One day, Gasparilla discovered a place filled with great hiding spots—Tampa Bay!

Price: $10.00
Paperback: 37 pages
Published: December 20, 2018
Language: English

ISBN-10: 1945812699
ISBN-13: 978-1945812699
Dimensions 8 x 0.1 x 10 in
Shipping Weight: 4.8 oz

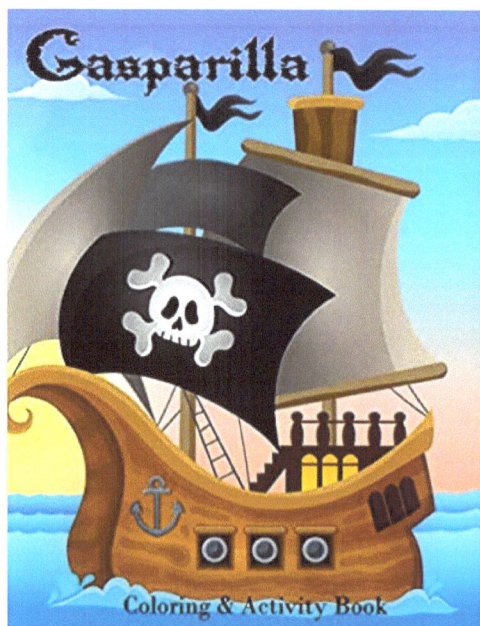

The Book on Retirement
Are You Ready for the Second Half of Your Financial Life?

By Kevin Houser, Gary Plessl

Are you really ready for retirement? If your plan for retirement has only been focused on savings and accumulation of assets, you are likely only half prepared for retirement. The real key to a comfortable retirement is what you do with those assets during the "Second Half" of your financial life, when the focus shifts from savings and accumulation to income and distribution.

Price: $19.95
Paperback: 130 pages
Published: March 20, 2015
Language: English

ISBN-10: 0692356681
ISBN-13: 978-0692356685
Dimensions 6 x 0.3 x 8.5 in
Shipping Weight: 7.3 oz

Dancing with Your Story from the Inside Out

By Arielle Giordano

A journey of transformation and being your authentic self through stories, dance, and writing.

Arielle Giordano empowers you to Dance Your Story from the Inside Out by freeing yourself through dance so that you may finally release your authentic truth and break the shackles of silence with your body's natural rhythms. At the end of each chapter, Giordano offers personal journaling and conscious reflection in conjunction with free-spirited dance. Giordano prescribes a practical means to self-discovery through fun and creative expressions. Together, the journaling, reflection, and dance assignments help unlock our stories and set our true selves free.

Price: $20.00
Paperback: 136 pages
Published: April 12, 2017
Language: English

ISBN-10: 1945812060
ISBN-13: 978-1945812064
Dimensions: 6 x 0.3 x 9 in
Shipping Weight: 9.3 oz

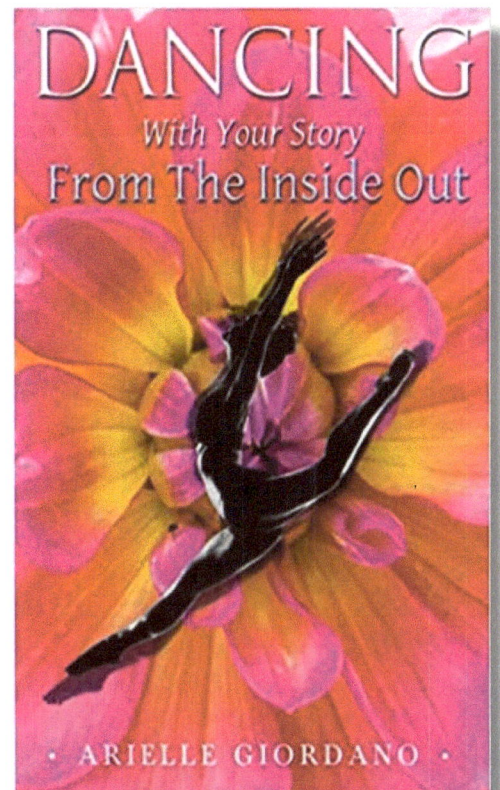

You Are Worthier

A Guide to Improving Your Illness or Injury on the Road to Recovery

By Jeanette Kildevæld

Recovering from a severe illness or injury can be an extremely difficult process. However, you are still worthy of fulfilling a life of happiness and success. Though the path to recovery may seem long and endless now—you are not alone. Let Jeanette Kildevaeld be your guide through the dark and hopeless times to reach a future where anything is possible.

Price: $20.00
Paperback: 202 pages
Published: May 23, 2017
Language: English

ISBN-10: 1945812109
ISBN-13: 978-1945812101
Dimensions 5.5 x 0.5 x 8.5 in
Shipping Weight: 11.4 oz

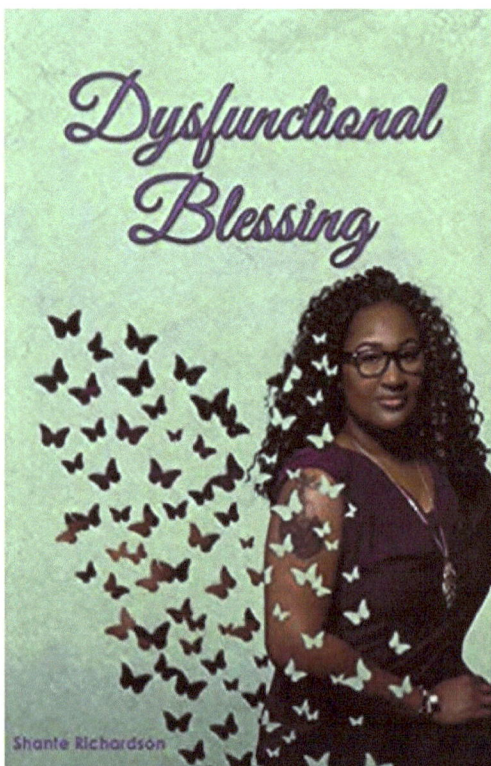

Dysfunctional Blessing

By Shanté Richardson

This book represents the journey of a woman who was battered through abusive relationships, had a child as a teen, endured homelessness, and betrayal. The stops along this road are markers of change and a vision of innocence slipping away. However, it is through this journey that faith is born, reborn, and finally understood. This is the story of a survivor.

Price: $15.00
Paperback: 138 pages
Published: May 23, 2017
Language: English

ISBN-10: 1945812117
ISBN-13: 978-1945812118
Dimensions 6 x 0.3 x 9 in
Shipping Weight: 9.3 oz

Gifts from a Glacier
The Quest for an American Flag and 52 Souls

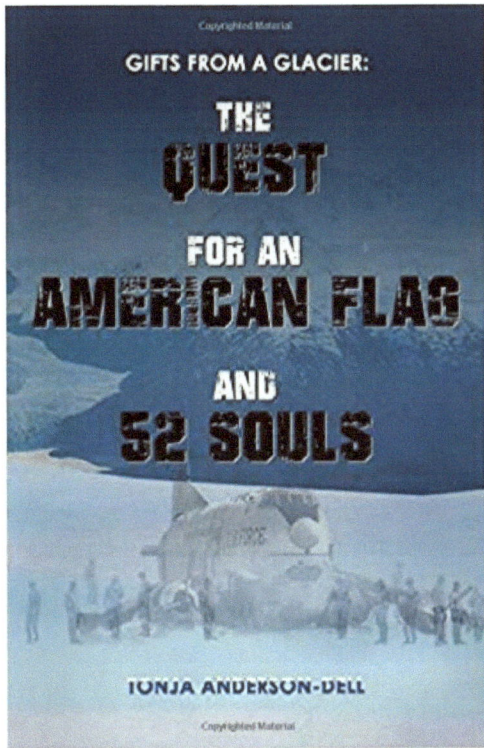

By Tonja Anderson

On November 22, 1952, 52 American soldiers departed on a C-124 Globemaster plane heading for Anchorage, Alaska. They never made it to their destination. When a rescue was deemed too expensive by the military, these men were left to the Alaskan wilderness and found their untimely demise. 60 years later, their true fate was still unknown to their loved ones and the world. Instead of living with this uncertainty, Tonja Anderson-Dell decides to take on the government to learn the secret of this disaster and return the bodies of the passengers from the C-124 Globemaster.

Price: $20.00
Paperback: 126 pages
Published: July 1, 2017
Language: English

ISBN-10: 1945812133
ISBN-13: 978-1945812132
Dimensions 6 x 0.3 x 9 in
Shipping Weight: 7 oz

Transitioning into Primary School
Your Passport to Success

By Carol D. Minnis

The objective of this book is to help the grade 1 student settle as quickly as possible, so he can be about the business of learning. Every school age child in the Commonwealth of the Bahamas, from Inagua in the South to Grand Bahamas in the North, will benefit from using this book. The student will learn: a) Ways to help himself successfully survive primary school, b) Study skills to perform better in school, c) Skills for building self-esteem, d) Skills for handling bullies, e) How to properly use the internet, and f) How to save money at an early age. These are valuable skills that should be beneficial to the grade 1 student for the rest of his/ her life.

Price: $20.00
Paperback: 74 pages
Published: July 10, 2017
Language: English

ISBN-10: 1945812087
ISBN-13: 978-1945812088
Dimensions 8.5 x 0.2 x 11 in
Shipping Weight: 8.8 oz

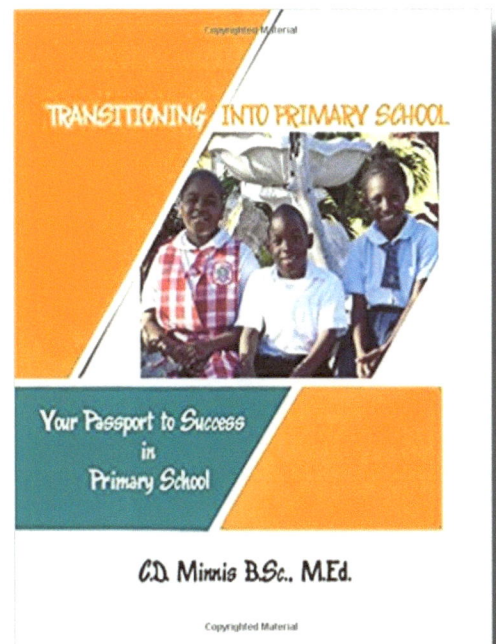

Transitioning into Junior High School
Your Passport for Surviving Junior High School

By Carol D. Minnis

The objective of this book is to help the grade 7 student settle as quickly as possible, so he/she can be about the business of learning. Every school age child in Junior High School, in the Commonwealth of The Bahamas, from Inagua in the south to Grand Bahama in the north, can benefit from using this book. The student will learn: a. Ways to help him/her successfully survive Junior High school. b. Study skills to perform better in school. c. Anger management and conflict resolution skills. d. How to properly use the internet. e. Money management skills at an early age. The grade 7 student will learn valuable skills that will benefit him/her for the rest of his/her life.

Price: $20.00
Paperback: 78 pages
Published: July 13, 2017
Language: English

ISBN-10: 1945812079
ISBN-13: 978-1945812071
Dimensions 8.5 x 0.2 x 11 in
Shipping Weight: 9.1 oz

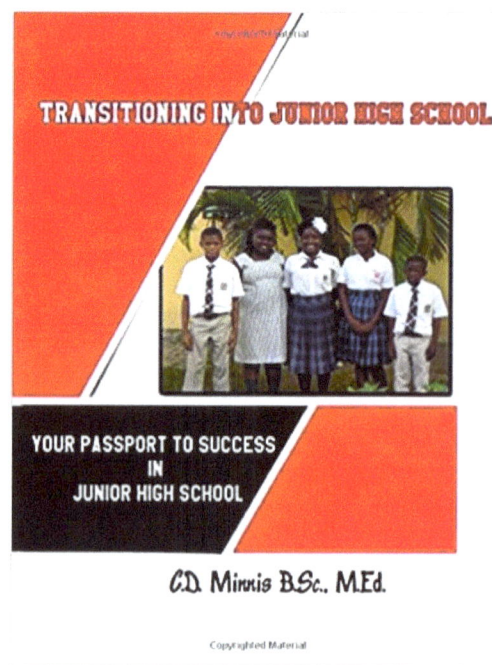

Transitioning into Senior High School
Your Passport to Success

By Carol D. Minnis

Every school age child in Senior High School, in the Commonwealth of The Bahamas, from Inagua in the south to Grand Bahama in the north, can benefit from using this book. The student will: a. Learn ways to help him/her successfully survive Senior High School. b. Learn how to improve study skills to perform better in school. c. Learn about graduation requirements to obtain The Bahamas High School Diploma. d. Learn useful Drug Awareness information. e. Learn how to use the internet properly. f. Find helpful information about sexuality. g. Learn money management skills.

Price: $20.00
Paperback: 86 pages
Published: July 17, 2017
Language: English

ISBN-10: 1945812095
ISBN-13: 978-1945812095
Dimensions 8.5 x 0.2 x 11 in
Shipping Weight: 9.9 oz

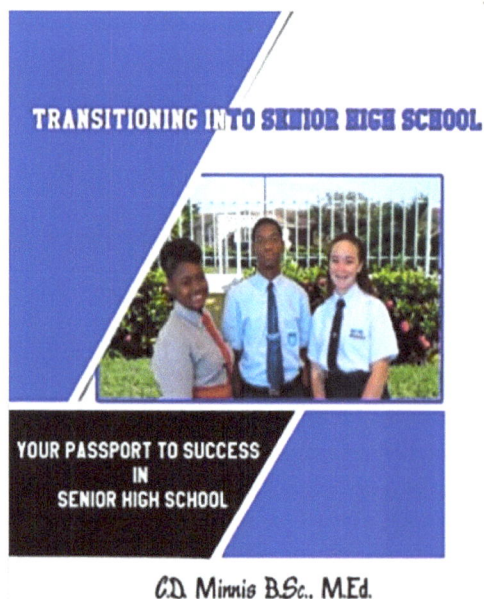

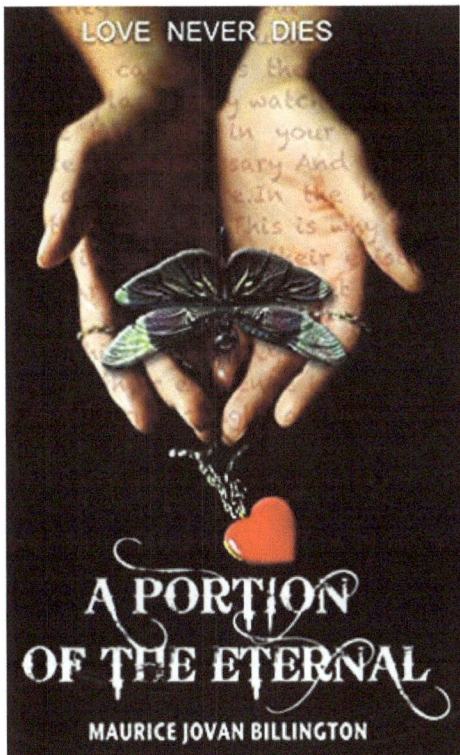

A Portion of the Eternal

By Maurice Jovan Billington

"A Portion of the Eternal" is a hauntingly beautiful novel about the mysterious death of a young boy and his girlfriend, Liv, who must continue to believe in love even in the wake of her overwhelming sadness. Winner of the Fade in Screenwriting Award for Best Thriller for his screenplay "9" and a poet, "This Plane Is Going To Crash," author Maurice Jovan Billington's story draws a reader in as a new student arrives in Liv's life bringing with him, redemption, revenge, or possibly both.

Price: $18.00
Paperback: 344 pages
Published: September 7, 2017
Language: English

ISBN-10: 1945812168
ISBN-13: 978-1945812163
Dimensions 6 x 0.8 x 9 in
Shipping Weight: 1.3 lbs

Morten and Gordon
Shelter from the Storm

By Donna L. Valentino, Ann Pilicer (Illustrator)

The story of two squirrels, brothers Morten and Gordon live on a farm and are loving it. Whether they are watching the farmer plant his crops or sampling them, they always seem to be living life to the fullest. One night, a storm comes and the brothers need to find shelter. Morten and Gordon scurry up to the farmer's porch and seek refuge from the weather in his warm boots, staying safe and dry all night long.

Price: $13.00
Paperback: 32 pages
Published: September 25, 2017
Language: English

ISBN-10: 194581215X
ISBN-13: 978-1945812156
Dimensions 8 x 0.1 x 10 in
Shipping Weight: 4.3 oz

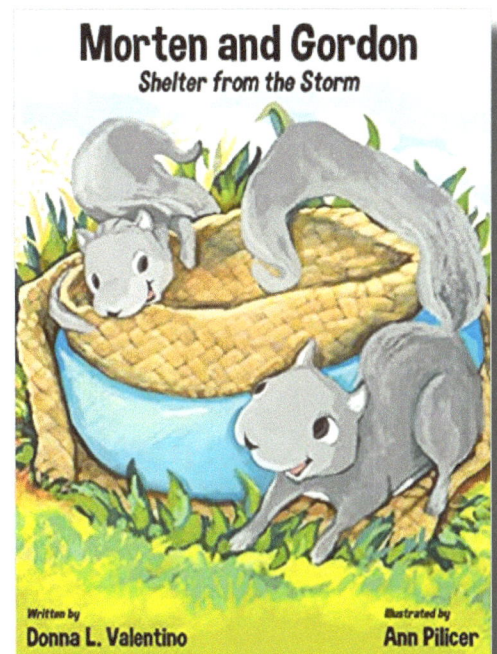

Scabs Heal All Wounds
True Story of a Replacement Player

By Edward Porcelli

On August 12th, 1994, the longest work stoppage in MLB history began. Edward Porcelli, author of "Scabs Heal All Wounds", tells the story of the strike from a replacement player's perspective during perhaps the darkest time in MLB history. From cancelling the World Series in 1994 and announcing the use of replacement players to President Bill Clinton demanding the executives of MLB and the MLBPA to come to an agreement, Mr. Porcelli gives a detailed chronology of events and how it affected the players, coaches, and management. His true story reveals behind the scenes interaction with minor league players' views on "crossing the line" and the ramifications of becoming a scab.

Price: $20.00
Paperback: 262 pages
Published: October 2, 2017
Language: English

ISBN-10: 1945812265
ISBN-13: 978-1945812262
Dimensions 5.5 x 0.6 x 8.5 in
Shipping Weight:14.2 oz

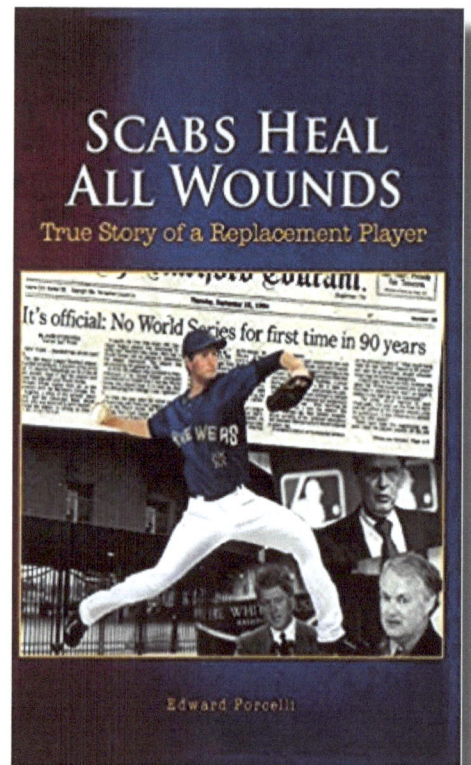

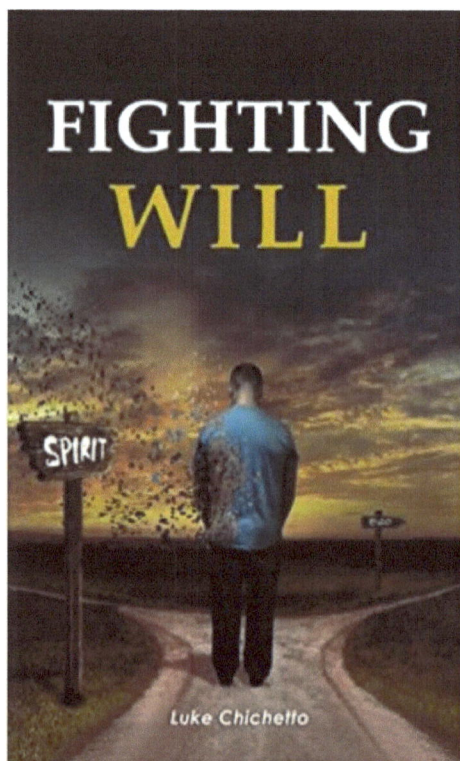

Fighting Will

By Luke Chichetto

One man's journey from being chained to an ego mindset, reinforced by working in the tough professional sports industry, to breaking free and evolving to a higher conscious and spirituality. After landing a dream job in the NFL, author Luke Chichetto still felt empty inside. Follow Luke's journey from having it all to losing it all and changing your mental state to find spiritual bliss.

Price: $20.00
Paperback: 172 pages
Published: October 3, 2017
Language: English

ISBN-10: 1945812176
ISBN-13: 978-1945812170
Dimensions 5 x 0.4 x 8 in
Shipping Weight: 8.8 oz

My "Everything" File
Everything My Loved Ones Need to Know About Me

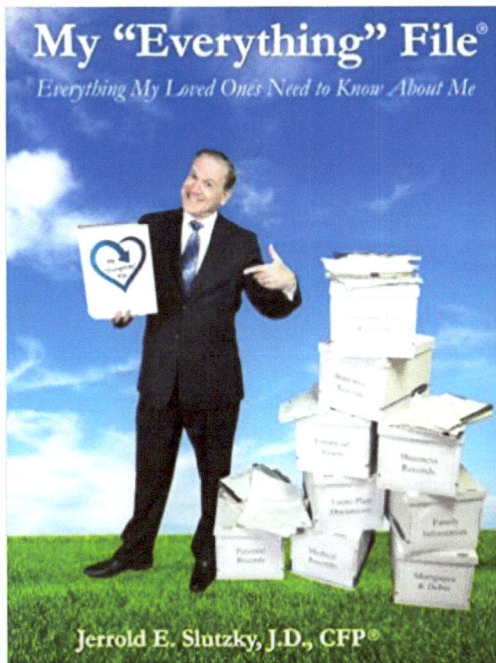

By Jerrold E. Slutzky

During our lives, we all accumulate a vast amount of information about every little aspect of our lives. It's a wonder we can remember it all! So, what happens if you become incapacitated or die? Who else knows all of the important details of your life? "My 'Everything' File" is intended to help you create a comprehensive document containing almost everything you would want your loved ones to know about you. This will enable them to take care of you and, if needed, handle your affairs if you become unable to do so yourself!

Price: $29.95
Paperback: 452 pages
Published: October 4, 2017
Language: English

ISBN-10: 1945812222
ISBN-13: 978-1945812224
Dimensions 8.5 x 1 x 11 in
Shipping Weight: 2.8 oz

In Defense of Adversity
Turning Your Toughest Challenges into Your Greatest Success

By Steve Gavatorta

In our high tech, fast-paced, rapidly changing world, adversity is hitting us at speeds significantly faster than ever—and at a younger age—leaving us little time to respond and arming us with far too few tools for controlling that response in a productive manner. It's easy for a person to become averse to risk and to become frustrated and afraid of things when he or she lacks the tools to handle them. In this Amazon Best Selling book, author Steve Gavatorta will give you the resources to survive in this ever-changing world.

Price: $15.99
Paperback: 190 pages
Published: October 24, 2017
Language: English

ISBN-10: 1945812206
ISBN-13: 978-1945812200
Dimensions 6 x 0.4 x 9 in
Shipping Weight: 9.1 oz

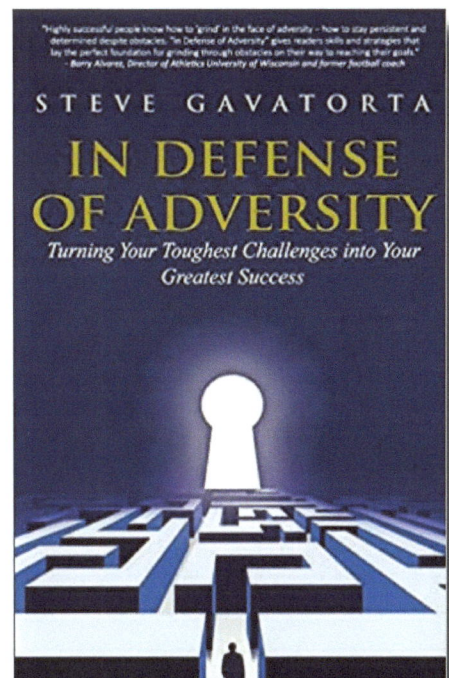

How to Catch a Shark

By Anthony Amos and Kevin Harrington

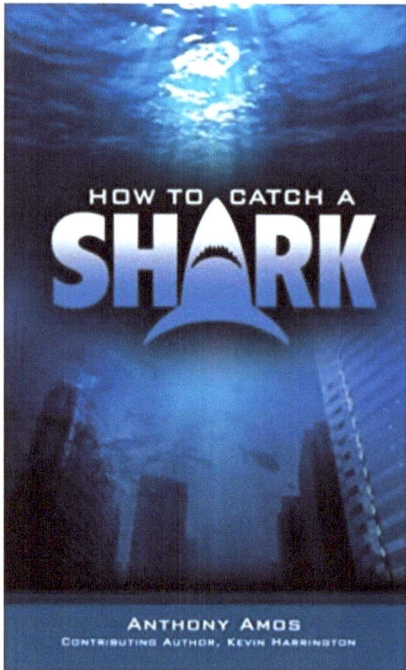

What is a shark in today's business world? Sharks are tough, self-made, multi-millionaire and billionaire tycoons and they are always searching for the best businesses and products that America has to offer. There is even a critically-acclaimed reality show called Shark Tank where entrepreneurs try to convince a panel of sharks to part with their own money and become investors in their company. This book describes how to get a shark interested in your company to change your business forever.

Price: $19.99
Paperback: 152 pages
Published: January 15, 2016
Language: English

ISBN-10: 0615971199
ISBN-13: 978-0615971193
Dimensions 5 x 0.35 x 8 in
Shipping Weight: 5.6 oz

Living Wisdom
Principles for a Life Well Lived

By Rev. Chad C. Fernald

What is it? How does a person discover it?

The Biblical books of wisdom contain a wealth of practical insight for the ordering of life based on sound principles which lead to healthy patterns for our personal lives, our homes and our communities. Living Wisdom: Principles for a Life Well Lived provides a framework for balanced, principle based living by exploring key areas of life in which God's Living Wisdom may be readily applied. Living Wisdom invites the reader to be challenged and changed by the straightforward teaching of Biblical Wisdom and confronts all with the call to be wise!

Price: $19.99
Paperback: 248 pages
Published: January 14, 2016
Language: English

ISBN-10: 0692602542
ISBN-13: 978-0692602546
Dimensions 5 x 0.6 x 8 in
Shipping Weight: 11.8 oz

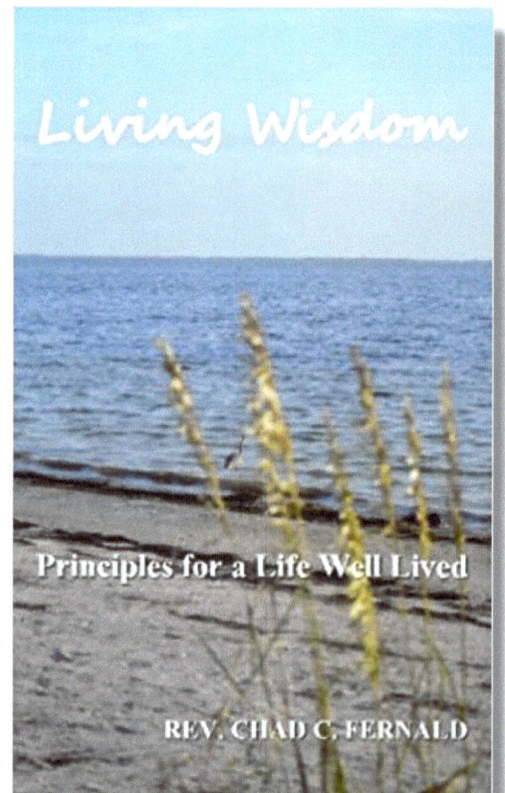

From Stand-Up Comedian to Stand-Up Teacher

By Mike Rivera, Craig Sidorowicz

From "Stand-up Comedian to Stand-up Teacher" is the story of Mike Rivera, "America's Most Hilarious Teacher." Talented and experienced in the worlds of both comedy and teaching, Mike brings together the unique perspectives of a nationally touring stand-up comedian, and an award-winning teacher, with the purpose of invigorating today's American classroom. He calls this "The Comedy/Teaching Craft" and "The STAND-UP Strategies."

Price: $19.99
Paperback: 150 pages
Published: February 9, 2016
Language: English

ISBN-10: 0692610863
ISBN-13: 978-0692610862
Dimensions 6 x 0.3 x 9 in
Shipping Weight: 9.9 oz

Over 40 & Sexy as Hell

By Robert Drapkin MD FAC, Donny Kim, Ashleigh Gass

The complete guide to diet, exercise, supplements, lifestyle training, and how your body works.

Price: $35.00
Paperback: 170 pages
Published: February 10, 2016
Language: English

ISBN-10: 0692626727
ISBN-13: 978-0692626726
Dimensions 6 x 0.4 x 9 in
Shipping Weight:11.4 oz

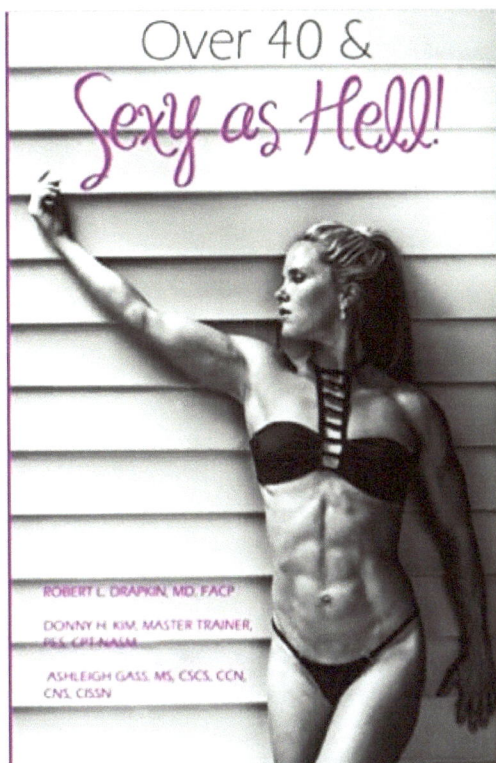

No Time to Care

A Leadership Game Plan to Ensure Caregiver Engagement

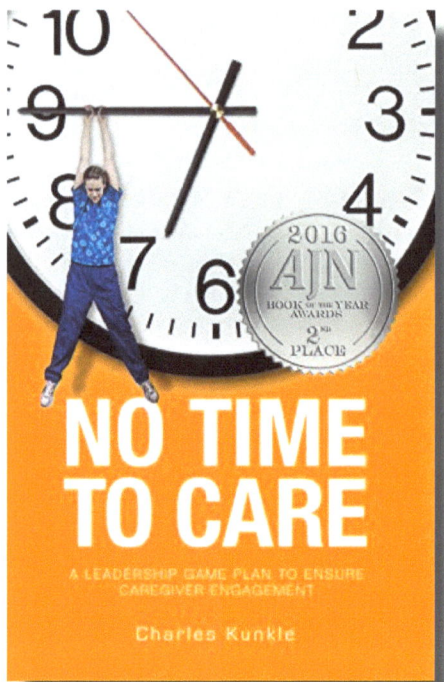

By Charles Kunkle

The American Journal of Nursing 2nd Place Award Winner of 2016!
In any hospital setting, a team of enthusiastic and engaged caregivers translates into better patient outcomes. But how can leaders foster engagement among workers who, all too often, are overwhelmed by the pressure to meet the needs of patients as well as the growing expectations of their employers in today's high-stress health-care environments? No Time to Care has the answer. Building on the core idea that patient satisfaction is the indirect measure of caregiver engagement, each chapter provides practical and cost-effective solutions that any leader can implement to help get all the bedside caregivers on the same page.

Price: $19.95
Paperback: 146 pages
Published: February 10, 2016
Language: English

ISBN-10: 0692614141
ISBN-13: 978-0692614143
Dimensions 6 x 0.3 x 9 in
Shipping Weight: 12.6 oz

Chasing Rainbows

Parallel Shades of Normality

By Prisqua Camiul

This is the story about two women who fight through the struggles of life in two completely different ways. One woman strives to keep a desperate grip on reality whilst the other immerses herself in a virtual escape to deal with her pain. From being a mother to finding love on the other side of the world, the story will take you on an emotional roller-coaster. Two worlds collide as we travel through time with them, sharing the laughter and tears.

Price: $19.99
Paperback: 302 pages
Published: April 21, 2016
Language: English

ISBN-10: 0692667245
ISBN-13: 978-0692667248
Dimensions 6 x 0.7 x 9 in
Shipping Weight: 1.2 lbs

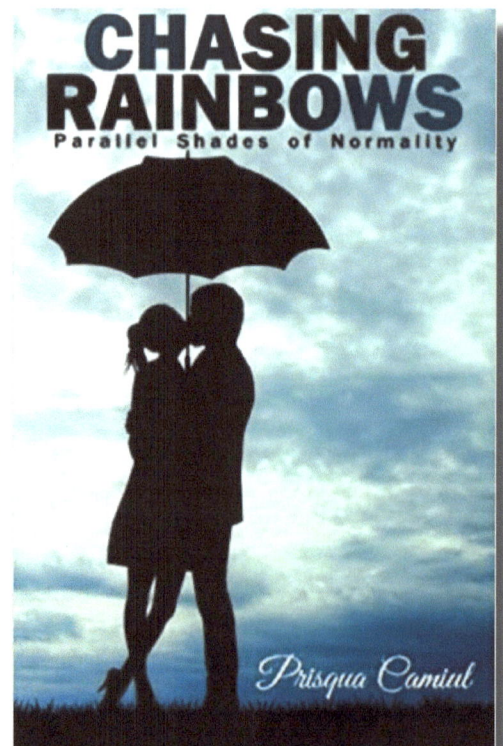

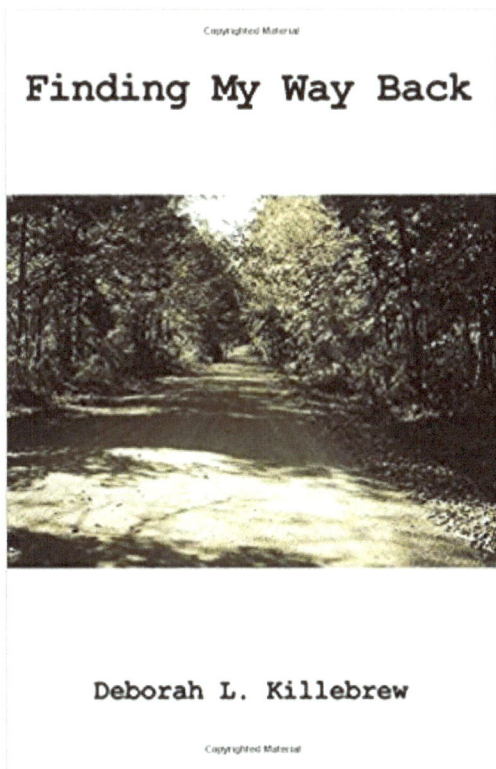

Finding My Way Back

By Deborah L. Killebrew

"A Tragic & Inspirational Story Told by a Woman Who Can Not Speak"
What if in the blink of an eye, you no longer were able to speak, walk, work, or dress yourself? What would you do if you could not even tell your children that you loved them? For Debbie Killebrew, these horrible questions came true in one night of drinking that changed her life forever. However, Debbie has fought to overcome the impossible, even when she was told that she would never walk again, never drive again, and never live a normal life again. Her inspiring true story will show you that no matter what twists and turns life takes, you can get up and keep going – and also serves as an unfortunately realistic testimony about how drinking and driving can truly take away everything you know.

Price: $20.00
Paperback: 232 pages
Published: August 31, 2016
Language: English

ISBN-10: 194581201X
ISBN-13: 978-1945812019
Dimensions 6 x 0.5 x 9 in
Shipping Weight:14.6 oz

Take A Breath
A Transplant Journey

By M.D., Karen A. Kelly

STOP. BREATHE.
In this true story, Dr. Karen A. Kelly M.D. shares her husband's journey through a life-saving lung transplant. Learning about his courageous battle can help any patient or caregiver understand the extensive responsibilities required for a successful organ transplant. As a pediatrician, Dr. Kelly found herself in a different role as caretaker not as provider. Her experience highlights the vital importance of taking care of oneself in order to adequately care for a sick loved one.

Price: $12.95
Paperback: 120 pages
Published: October 1, 2016
Language: English

ISBN-10: 1945812044
ISBN-13: 978-1945812040
Dimensions 5 x 0.3 x 8 in
Shipping Weight: 4.6 oz

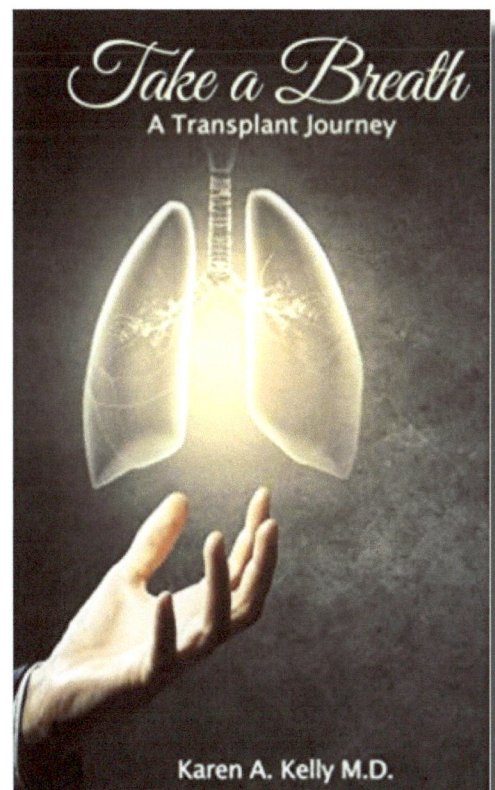

Become the MVP in Your Industry by Surfing the Radio Waves

By Brandon Rimes, Connor Anthony

Within their book, Become the MVP in Your Industry by Surfing the Radio Waves, Brandon Rimes and Connor Anthony dive into all of the details of running your own radio show. Each key guides hungry entrepreneurs to create a radio show that not only boosts business and networking contacts, but also creates another income stream. The two men share their knowledge of the radio industry to empower those who wish to take their career to the next level. Learn how to become the pioneer of your industry by utilizing a less traveled path that offers endless opportunities.

Price: $20.00
Paperback: 144 pages
Published: October 3, 2016
Language: English

ISBN-10: 1945812001
ISBN-13: 978-1945812002
Dimensions 6 x 0.3 x 9 in
Shipping Weight: 9.6 oz

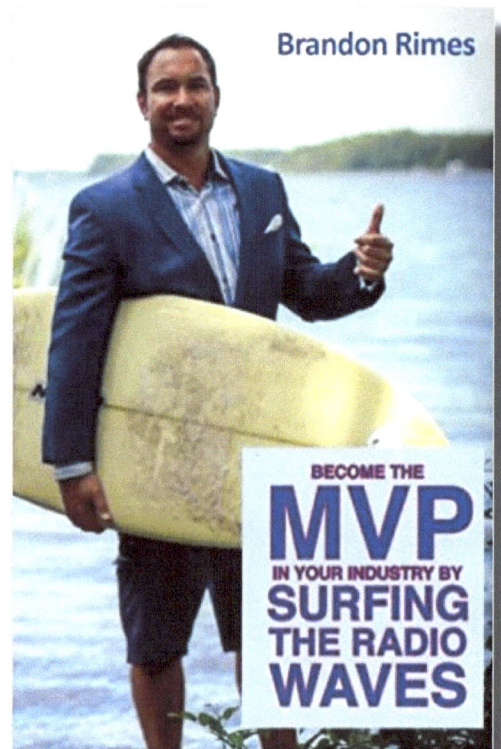

Brandon Rimes

BECOME THE
MVP
IN YOUR INDUSTRY BY
SURFING
THE RADIO
WAVES

Flies in My Coffee

IT'S GOOD TO BE THE
QUEEN

M. Rene Harris

Flies In My Coffee

By M. Rene Harris

Amazon Best Seller and 2016 Most Inspirational Story! If you could only fit what you need into three boxes to start your life over, what would you take? That's what one woman was faced with when she decided to pack up what she could for herself and four children to leave a toxic situation. You never know what you're capable of surviving until you are faced with it. Fight or flight. What would you do?

Price: $20.00
Paperback: 232 pages
Published: October 4, 2016
Language: English

ISBN-10: 1945812028
ISBN-13: 978-1945812026
Dimensions 5.5 x 0.5 x 8.5 in
Shipping Weight:12.8 oz

From the Farm to the Boardroom
Leadership Lessons

By Rita Lowman

From the small town of Columbus, Georgia to the big city of Tampa Bay, Florida, Rita Lowman has plowed her own path. Her story takes readers on a journey of strength, tenacity, and drive that has bucked the idea of a simple job and replaced it with a brilliant career. Her roots in a small town gave her the courage and the strength to keep pushing through the herd and taking her place at the head of the Florida banking industry.

Price: $15.00
Paperback: 120 pages
Published: December 1, 2016
Language: English

ISBN-10: 1945812036
ISBN-13: 978-1945812033
Dimensions 6 x 0.3 x 9 in
Shipping Weight: 7.2 oz

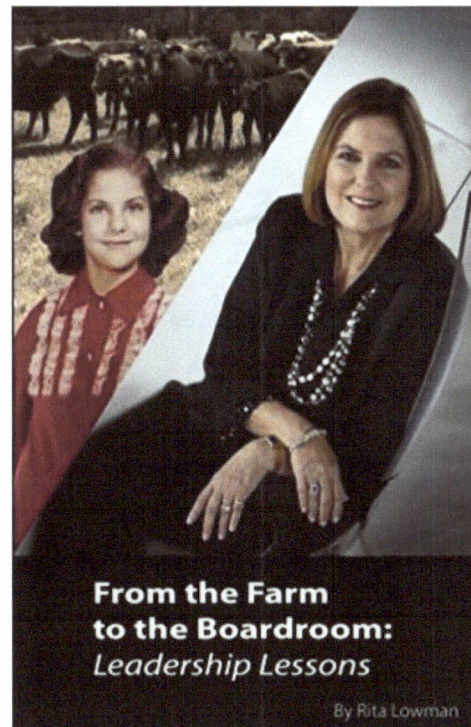

From the Farm to the Boardroom: *Leadership Lessons*

By Rita Lowman

Nothing Happens Until the Meeting is Set
Connecting People, Business & Products

By John McKee

business453

Nothing Happens Until The Meeting Is Set

John McKee
Connecting People, Business & Product

John McKee, best known for his 26 years in new Business Development with over 25,000 sales call meetings and expertise with connecting people, businesses and products now identifies his passion while writing his story. After inventing his first product Cosmo Finger Guard, then reading Key Person of Influence, he now shares his story that defines his niche as a KPI. John now shares his knowledge to help Entrepreneurs and Business Startup's through their quest to gain new customers and generate sales leads with his new book. He is convinced that B2B Selling is the number one missing component in growing business.

Price: $24.95
Paperback: 230 pages
Published: July 8, 2016
Language: English

ISBN-10: 0692737677
ISBN-13: 978-0692737675
Dimensions 5.5 x 0.5 x 8.5 in
Shipping Weight:12.6 oz

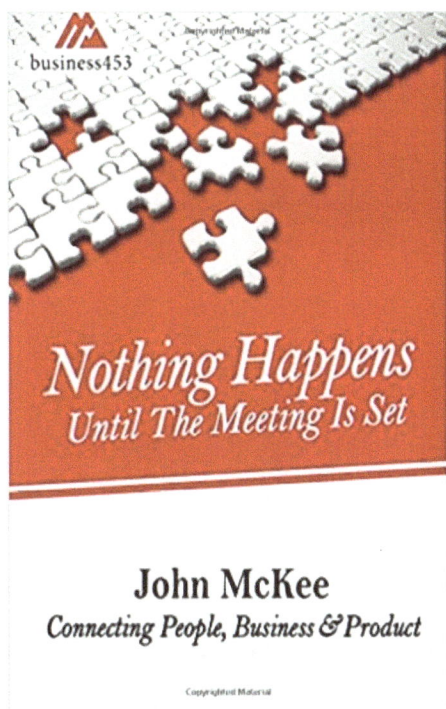

Launch Your Book into the Stratosphere & be a Best Seller (Volume 4)

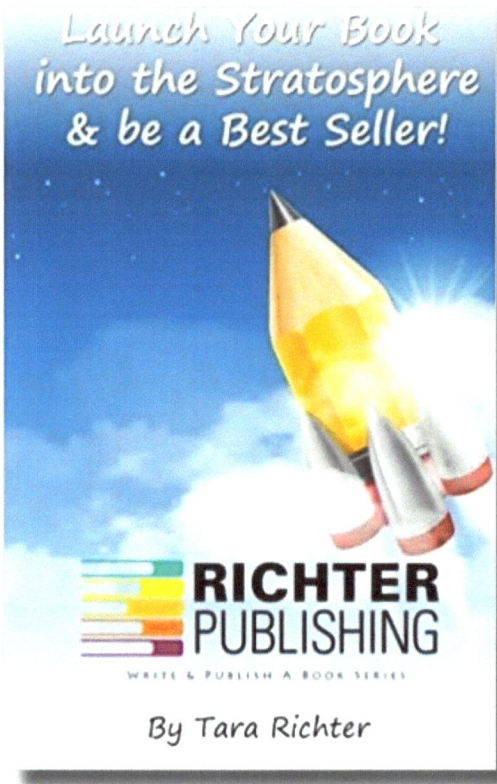

By Tara Richter

Learn the 10 crucial ingredients to launch your book successfully & become a best seller! Within this book you will discover how to; market your book, utilize SEO to get your party ranking high in Google searches, get media attention, draw a crowd to your event, why old book signings are out dated, what the new techniques are and become a best-selling author!

Price: $14.99
Paperback: 80 pages
Published: April 9, 2015
Language: English

ISBN-10: 0692425330
ISBN-13: 978-0692425336
Dimensions 6 x 0.2 x 9 in
Shipping Weight: 12.6 oz

The 3 Pillars of Strength
Improving Your Pysical, Mental and Spiritual Fitness

By Jeffrey White

It's important to understand that shortcomings in one aspect of your life could have a ripple effect and drastically affect other aspects. Many of us tend to focus on our spirituality, while neglecting our physical health. Others demean themselves and lose all self-respect in the quest for money or success. Instead of dealing with their issues head on, some will abuse alcohol, drugs, or engage in other harmful activities in hopes of avoiding the situation. The purpose of this book is to help you become physically, mentally and spiritually fit— simultaneously—with each aspect of fitness having its own section.

Price: $22.95
Paperback: 282 pages
Published: April 29, 2015
Language: English

ISBN-10: 0692424776
ISBN-13: 978-0692424773
Dimensions 6 x 0.6 x 9 in
Shipping Weight: 1.1 lbs

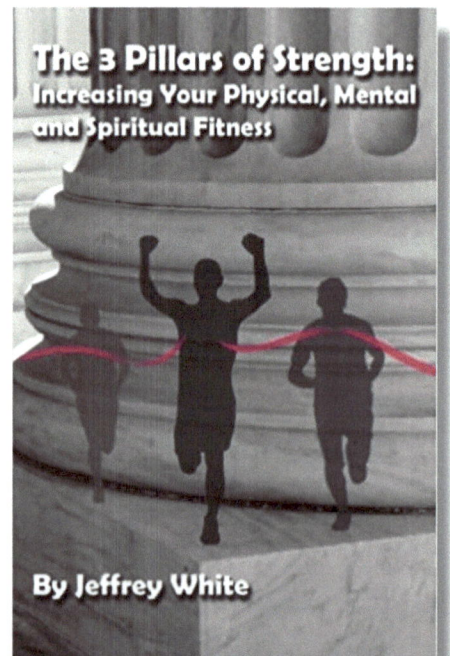

OMG! WTF? What's the Focus

A Guide for Building an Actionable Business Plan

By Ford Kyes, Barb Kyes, Juliet Kyes

usiness owners who are new to being coached and having a plan always have a lot in common in the way they operate and struggle to find focus. This book is a collaboration of three coaches who have worked directly with business owners in the last several years assisting them with putting their goals on paper and creating a lasting impact on the growth of their businesses. This book is meant to serve as a guide to assist you in forming an operational plan for your company. A specifically targeted, goal-oriented plan that both engages and inspires you—something you can compile all on one sheet of paper to run your weekly schedule based on your future annual and 90-day goals. Once your focus and a clear plan is set in place with your team, attaining the results you want will happen much quicker than it has in the past for your business.

Price: $27.97
Paperback: 206 pages
Published: May 27, 2015
Language: English

ISBN-10: 0692443290
ISBN-13: 978-0692443293
Dimensions 6 x 0.5 x 9 in
Shipping Weight:13.1 oz

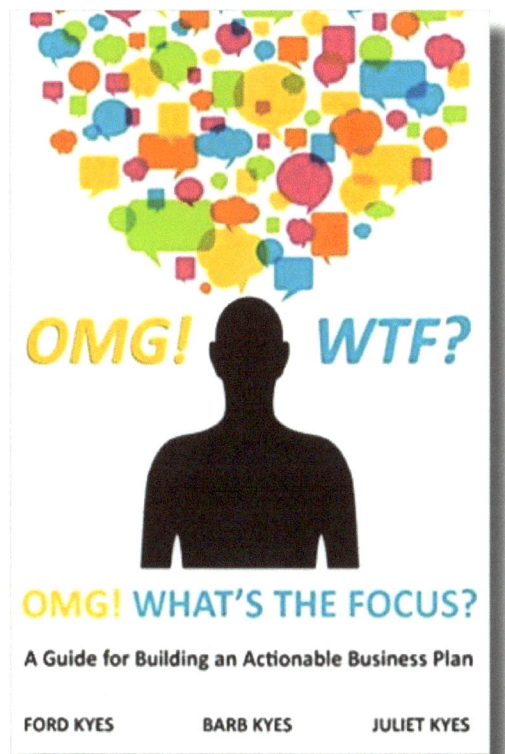

Plaintiff 101

The Black Book of Inside Information Your Lawyer Will Want You to Know

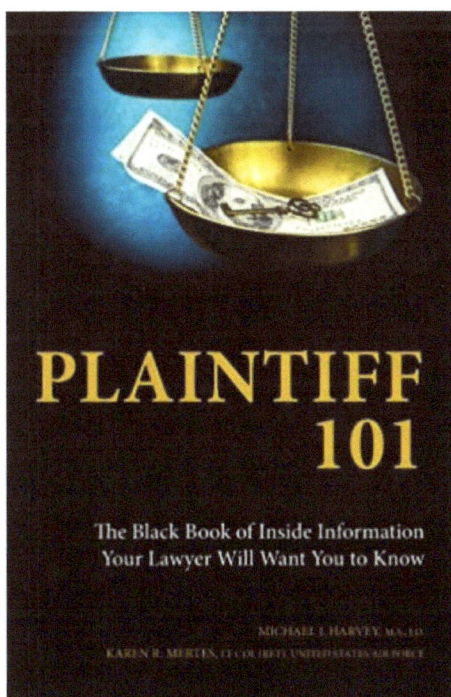

By Karen R. Mertes, Michael J. Harvey

#1 Amazon Best Seller! As seen on Daytime TV, ABC & Bay News 9
As my life hung in the balance after a tragic car accident caused by a drunk driver, I promised to spend the rest of my life helping others if I were to survive. Despite sustaining a traumatic brain injury, I am the founder and president of Fulfill Your Destiny, Inc., a 501(c)(3) non-profit dedicated to helping people whose careers have been altered by injury or other unforeseen circumstances. This book is to help other personal injury survivors contemplating litigation, or already involved in litigation. We're hopeful that plaintiffs' attorneys will see the benefit of providing this book as a teaching tool to their clients so as a team you can win your case!

Price: $24.95
Paperback: 126 pages
Published: September 14, 2015
Language: English

ISBN-10: 0692479619
ISBN-13: 978-0692479612
Dimensions 6 x 0.3 x 9 in
Shipping Weight: 8.6 oz

Modern IV Wellness

By Dr. Uhuru Smith MD, Dr. Tracy Edward Smith PhD

Modern IV wellness is the first book of its kind to introduce the world to the modern spin on the age-old use of IV therapy. IV vitamin and nutrient therapy has been around for decades used mostly by celebrities and the very wealthy. IV therapy is used commonly for anti-aging, as it improves the complexion and reversed dark spots and fine lines. IV therapy is used by weekend warriors and professional athletes to recover more quickly and avoid injury.

Price: $9.99
Paperback: 102 pages
Published: September 22, 2015
Language: English

ISBN-10: 0692520562
ISBN-13: 978-0692520567
Dimensions 5 x 0.2 x 8 in
Shipping Weight: 5.9 oz

Pink Hell
Breast Cancer Sucks

By Dr. Melissa Bailey

Dr. Melissa Bailey shares her personal story of battling breast cancer. A "Seinfeld" like story of her adventures dealing with all the ups and downs of the disease. She helps the reader bring a bit of humor to the otherwise dark periods of life. "Pink Hell" is a unique twist of fate as Melissa is a doctor, but never thought she would have to deal with cancer. The book inspires women of all ages to give hope that you too can overcome anything.

Price: $24.99
Paperback: 234 pages
Published: September 23, 2015
Language: English

ISBN-10: 0692533680
ISBN-13: 978-0692533680
Dimensions 6 x 0.5 x 9 in
Shipping Weight: 12.3 oz

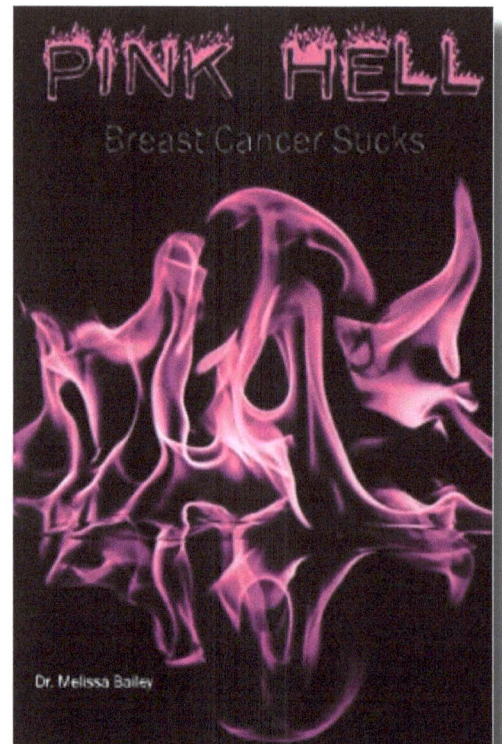

The Little Amazonian

By Miroslava Espinosa

In The Little Amazonian, Miroslava Espinosa tells us a modern-day survival story that will amaze. Told through her memories, she relates stories of close encounters with wild animals, struggle for education, food, and money, and a myriad of health issues. Through it all, she emerges a strong woman who faces all odds with renewed determination. Sold in English and Spanish (Spanish available in Hardback).

Price: $20.00
Paperback: 166 pages
Published: September 28, 2015
Language: English

ISBN-10: 0692531831
ISBN-13: 978-0692531839
Dimensions 5.5 x 0.4 x 8.5 in
Shipping Weight: 7.2 oz

Also available in Spanish!

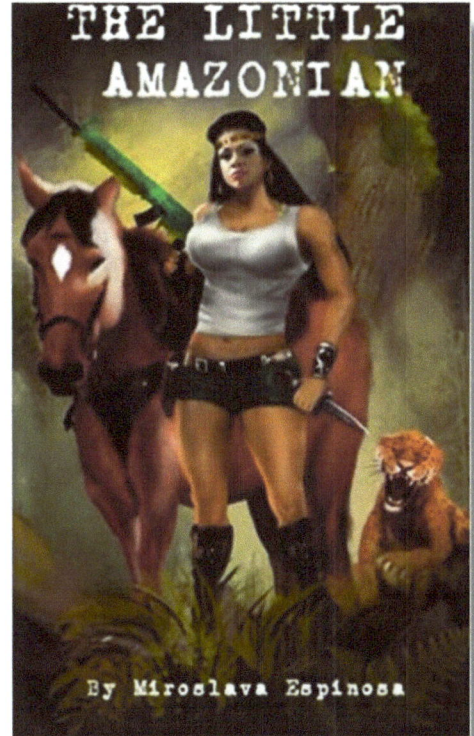

A Voice Crying in the Wilderness

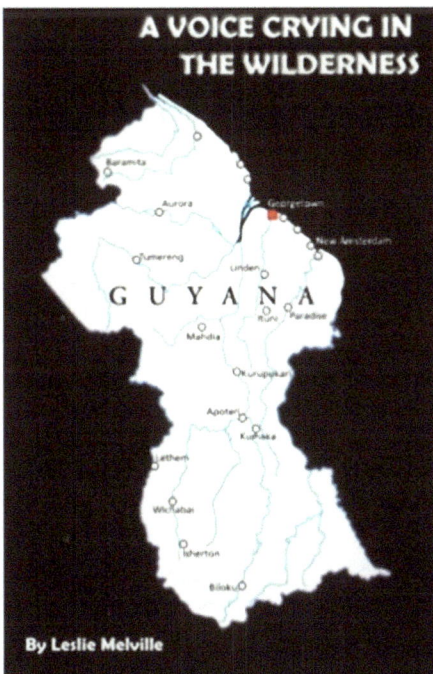

By Leslie Melville

As a world-renowned Trade Unionist, Mr. Melville often shared his forward-thinking views on the requirements for a successful relationship between the Union, the Employer, the Worker, and the Government. Mr. Melville viewed this relationship as a partnership with each side making an equally valuable contribution. This book is a compilation of fifteen thought provoking articles delivered throughout his career on various topics relating the relationship among the worker, the Corporation and the Government.

Price: $19.99
Paperback: 302 pages
Published: September 30, 2015
Language: English

ISBN-10: 0692461922
ISBN-13: 978-0692461921
Dimensions 6 x 0.7 x 9 in
Shipping Weight: 1.2 lbs

Stand

By Gary Hartfield

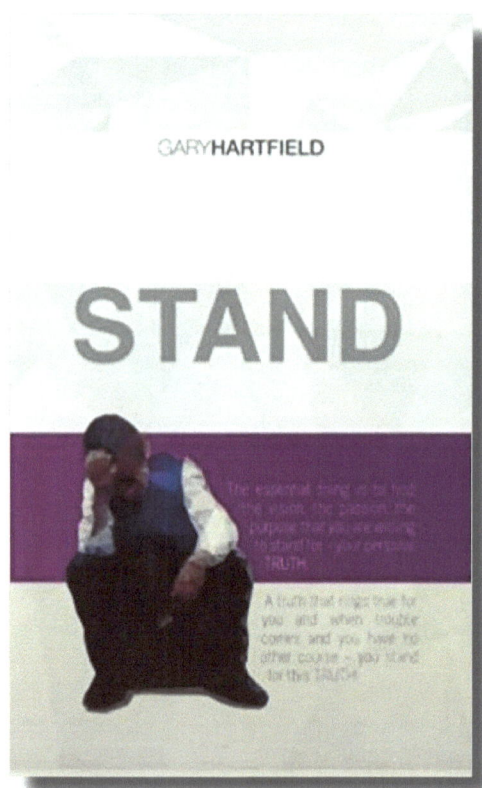

As the President and CEO of Serenity Village Inc, Serenity Village Insurance & Consulting and Sweet Talk Wireless, Gary Hartfield is passionate about bettering his community and sharing his experiences to inspire others. His compassion for others led him to launch Serenity Village Inc., which consists of several assisted living communities in Florida, and Serenity Village Insurance and Consulting, LLC. He has since gone on to invest in and launch several startups, one of which is Sweet Talk Wireless. His business acumen has helped him turn his ideas and passions into reality and grow his businesses and their success.

Price: $14.99
Paperback: 138 pages
Published: October 31, 2015
Language: English

ISBN-10: 0692549579
ISBN-13: 978-0692549575
Dimensions 5 x 0.3 x 8 in
Shipping Weight: 7.4 oz

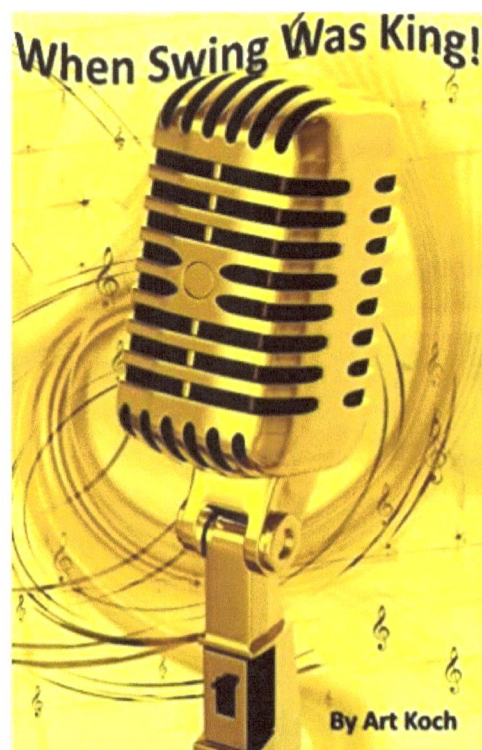

When Swing Was King

By Art Koch

Looking back at one of the most historical eras in America and American music. Throughout the history of the United States, music has always been a big part of the fabric that was woven to create the canvas that shaped this country. The author takes you on a journey from the minuet during the early days of our country's birth, to the turn of century with the waltz through ragtime and blues into the explosion of the 1950's with the birth of "rock-and-roll!"

Price: $14.99
Paperback: 102 pages
Published: November 30, 2015
Language: English

ISBN-10: 0692581723
ISBN-13: 978-0692581728
Dimensions 6 x 0.3 x 9 in
Shipping Weight: 7.4 oz

Publish A Book Yourself
Richter Publishing Volume 2

By Tara Richter

Your manuscript is done, edited, and you're ready to get it out to the world! Self-publishing is the quickest easiest way to get your book in people's hands. You have complete control over how it looks inside and out. I will walk you through the steps of how to: create a book cover, publish a finished book, format your manuscript for a digital book, and set up your payments and royalties. (So you too can feel like royalty!)

Price: $14.99
Paperback: 80 pages
Published: September 16, 2014
Language: English

ISBN-10: 0692295208
ISBN-13: 978-0692295205
Dimensions 6 x 0.2 x 9 in
Shipping Weight: 6.1 oz

Publish a Book Yourself!

RICHTER PUBLISHING
WRITE & PUBLISH A BOOK SERIES

By Tara Richter

Write a Book in 4 Weeks
Richter Publishing Volume 3

By Tara Richter

Discover how to write your own book in as little as 4 weeks. Yes, it can be done! Utilize these methods to get the words out of your head and onto paper. Filled with resources such as book outlines, writing challenge calendars, how to develop characters, stories and plot. Written by an award-winning author and publisher of 30 Amazon Best Sellers.

Price: $12.00
Paperback: 90 pages
Published: September 21, 2014
Language: English

ISBN-10: 0692298940
ISBN-13: 978-0692298947
Dimensions 6 x 0.2 x 9 in
Shipping Weight: 5.6 oz

Write a Book in 4 Weeks

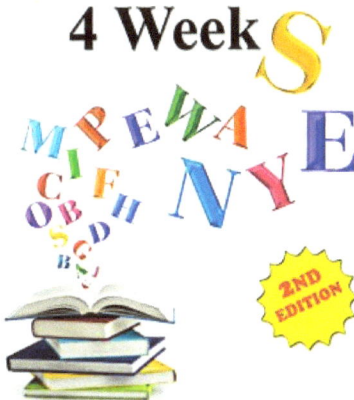

2ND EDITION

RICHTER PUBLISHING
WRITE & PUBLISH A BOOK SERIES

By Tara Richter

Blog Your Book into Existence
Richter Publishing Volume 1

Blog Your Book into Existence!

RICHTER PUBLISHING
WRITE & PUBLISH A BOOK SERIES

By Tara Richter

By Tara Richter

A blog is the easiest and quickest way to drive traffic to your website, your company, and your products. It gets you ranked high in Google if done properly and is also a functional way to write your book. I will walk you through the steps of how to: start a blog, use keywords for SEO, organize your blogs for your book, and get 4,000 organic hits a month. (Organic means free, in case you were thinking of non-hormone injected chicken breasts!)

Price: $9.99
Paperback: 62 pages
Published: August 20, 2014
Language: English

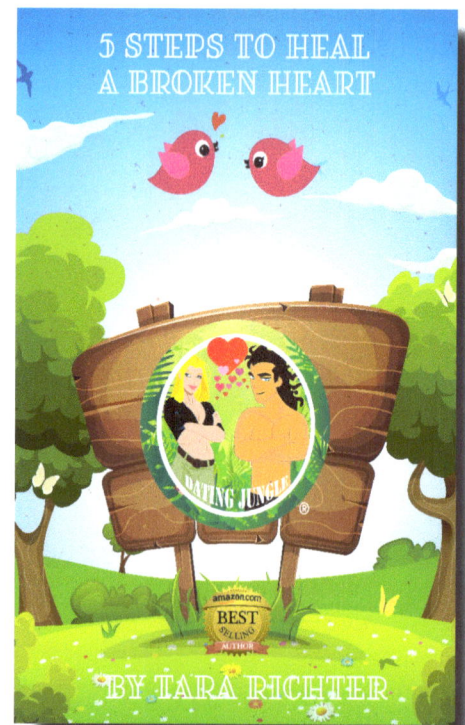

ISBN-10: 0692275908
ISBN-13: 978-0692275900
Dimensions 6 x 0.1 x 9 in
Shipping Weight: 5.1 oz

5 Steps to Heal A Broken Heart
The Dating Jungle Book 3

By Tara Richter

You don't have suffer in silence anymore. Download my guide that are proven methods to help you stop beating yourself up and the terrible pain that comes with a broken heart. I wrote this guide for myself as I too have just suffered from a broken heart. It's not easy, but you can learn from your pain, embrace it and grow from it. There is life after a broken heart.

Kindle Price: $9.99
Pages: 95
Published: June 8, 2013

Sold by: Amazon Digital
Language: English

5 STEPS TO HEAL A BROKEN HEART

DATING JUNGLE

amazon.com BEST SELLING AUTHOR

BY TARA RICHTER

10 Rules to Survive
the Internet Dating Jungle
The Dating Jungle Series 2

By Tara Richter

Welcome to the technology dating jungle! Utilize Certified Dating Coach, Tara Richter's, 10 rules to help you navigate your way through internet dating sites to find your loving Jane or Tarzan. Within this book you will be able to: brush up on internet dating terminology, get a comprehensive review of dating websites, weeding out dates online, how to take your online romance offline safely, build self-esteem, find healthy relationships, discover your jungle personality, funny real internet dating stories and more! Plus you can see more real-time information on The Dating Jungle's blog, website, Facebook and more! Just visit www.datingjunglebook.com.

Kindle Price: $4.99
Pages: 191 pages
Published: April 11, 2013

Sold by: Amazon Digital
Language: English

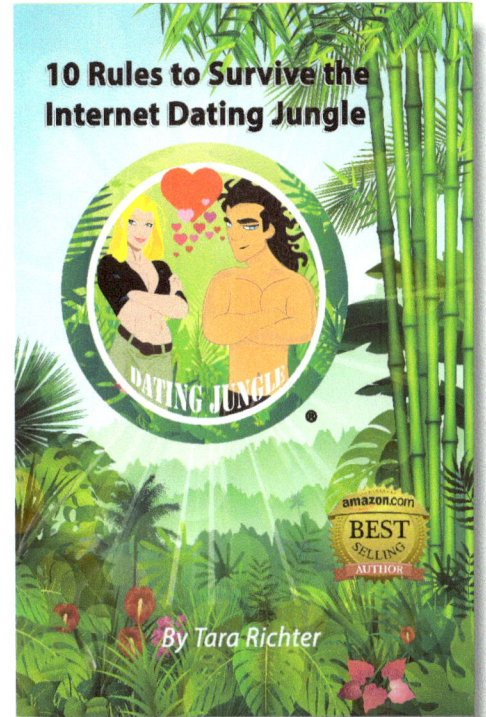

10 Rules to Survive the Dating Jungle
Dating Jungle Series Book 1

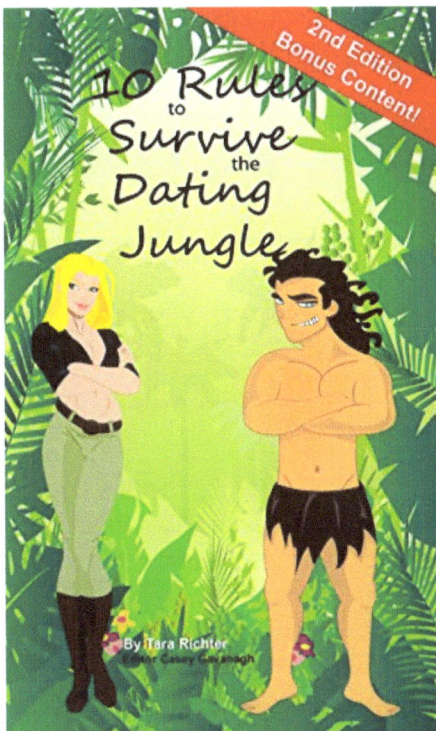

By Tara Richter

You've entered the dating Jungle! I know, it's a bit scary out here. Doesn't matter if you have just got divorced, had a bad break-up or starting to date for the first time. It's not easy venturing out into the dating world. Within the book you'll discover how to become more approachable, learn the art of flirting & how to keep your dating anxiety under control. Use the 10 Rules to take control of your dating life today!

Kindle Price: $4.99
File Size: 3736 KB
Published: November 14, 2013

ISBN-10: 0692623485
Sold by: Amazon Digital
Language: English

Writing Retreats in Peru!

Do you have a book inside of you, but don't have time to put pen to paper? Does the constant time restraints of daily life get in the way of your writing schedule? Have you been writing your book for 10 years, but it's just jumbled notes here and there and doesn't really resemble anything that really looks like a book? Do you love to travel the world but afraid to do it alone? Are you sick of being trapped in lock down and ready to explore the world? If you said yes to any of these questions, then a writing retreat is perfect for you! Tara Richter, the President of Richter Publishing, has traveled to over 45 different countries and published over 100 books. She is now combining both of her passions into writing retreats! In 2019 she left Florida, hopped on a plan solo to joined 17 strangers in Vietnam and lived in Asia for four months volunteering at nonprofits, immersing in the cultures and hanging out with elephants. They country hopped from Vietnam, Thailand, Japan and then Tara left the group and went on her own to Singapore and back to Thailand because she loved it so much. During this time she created the writing retreats, but the universe had other plans. Covid. So she had to put her dreams on hold, until now.

Tara is so excited to get back to exploring this awesome planet and helping people share their stories with the world. The writing retreats will be a small group of like minded people who want to get out of their comfort zone, explore new cultures and also work on their book. If you are a

writer, you know how difficult it is to focus on writing when you are in your normal daily grind. There are so many things that distract you. This retreat will take you out of your element and allow you the time to focus, plus utilize Tara's proven methods over the years to help you finally get your manuscript done!

Our first writing retreat is going to take place in Peru! It is going to be seven days long. It will be held from September 2nd until September 8th 2023. And it includes staying in luxurious hotels in the Sacred Valley and Cusco to explore all the amazing heritage that Peru has to offer. Read below to see all the details of our writing retreat to get your creative juices flowing on your next book!

2023 Retreat Itinerary!

DAY 1 - 9/02/2023: YOU ARRIVE IN LIMA

You fly into Lima airport. A representative will meet you at the airport and escort you to your hotel room. Included in the price is your stay at the airport hotel that night so we can all start our amazing trip together!

DAY 2 - 9/03/2023: LIMA – CUSCO – SACRED VALLEY – Shaman Despacho Ceremony

We will have a group breakfast at the hotel in the morning. Afterwards we will catch our short flight to the Inca capital city of Cusco together. Our guides and driver will pick you up from the airport in Cusco and embark upon a guided excursion through snowcapped mountains to the legendary Sacred Valley, it's as majestic today as it was during the reign of the Incas. We will stop along the way for a traditional lunch. You will see Inca terracing that climbs the steep valley walls and the beautiful temples of Pisac which inspire panoramic views of the jagged granite mountains. Pisac is the location for one of the best textile markets in the Andes. We continue into our luxurious resort in the Sacred Valley pictured above. A local Shaman will greet you from Peru, and you will have the chance to participate in a traditional "despacho" ceremony, giving gratitude to Mother Earth, and asking for a fruitful journey for all participants. This is a colorful experience to conjure up creative thoughts! Take the evening to relax and acclimate to the altitude. Dinner on your own.

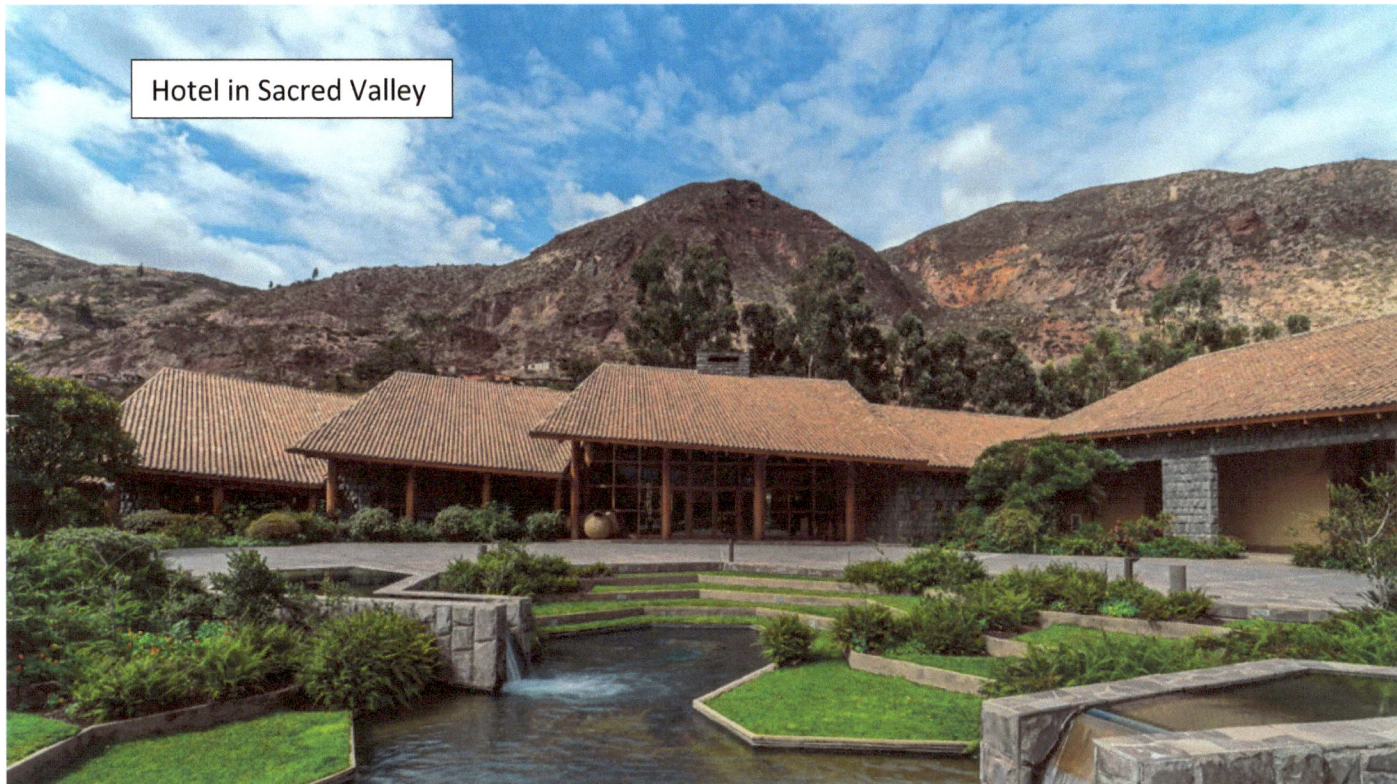

Hotel in Sacred Valley

DAY 3 - 9/04/2023: MORNING WORKSHOP #1 HOW TO WRITE A BOOK IN 4 WEEKS & BECOME AN EXPERT IN YOUR INDUSTRY

Enjoy a group breakfast at the resort. Workshop #1 from 9am-12pm. Enjoy lunch on your own at the resort. Surrounded by amazing mountains for inspiration, take time to work on your manuscript during the afternoon and enjoy the resort amenities. Schedule one on one time with Tara. Everyone will get a private one hour consultation during the retreat. Then a group dinner.

DAY 4 - 9/05/2023: MACHU PICCHU

After a group breakfast, we will take the train to Machu Picchu Town (Aguas Calientes.) This beautiful train ride traverses along the Vilcabamba River for 1 1/2 hours – and you will get to experience the "eyebrow of the jungle". Follow your English-speaking guides on an incredible tour of Machu Picchu. You will explore the famous ruins of this magnificent mountain citadel and learn about the history of the ancient people who created it. This afternoon we head to the train station for a ride back to Ollantaytambo where your private transportation will take you to Cusco where you will check in to your next fabulous hotel.

DAY 5 - 9/05/2023 WORKSHOP #2 ALL THE ELEMENTS THAT GO INTO A BOOK (*FICTION/ NONFICTION & CHILDREN'S*)

Breakfast at the hotel together. Workshop #2 from 9am -12pm. Free time during the afternoon to write in your book and explore the quaint streets of Cusco on your own. Return to hotel, where as a group we will walk to a fantastic restaurant for our dinner together.

DAY 6 - 09/07/2023 – WORKSHOP #3 – BOOK LEGAL STUFF, THE IMPORTANT & NOT SO FUN STUFF

Enjoy a group breakfast at the hotel. Workshop #3, 9am-12pm. Then a guided walking tour through Cusco's craft markets. You will visit the colonial cathedral and Koricancha, the Inca's Temple of the Sun and the main plaza, the Plaza de Armas. Experience the vibrancy of local neighborhoods. You will be returned to you hotel for another evening in colonial Cusco. Meet with the group for an included dinner at the end of the day.

DAY 7 - 09/08/2023 – WORKSHOP #4 DESIGNING A GREAT COVER & HIRING EDITORS – START THE JOURNEY HOME

After one last wonderful breakfast together, we will meet as a group to conclude our workshop. Then share lunch after the final workshop and depart from the hotel. The private driver will take you to the airport where you will catch your flight to Lima. You can stay in Lima and make your trip longer at the point, or you can make your connecting flight home. But the retreat is done. You will have all your amazing experiences, writing materials and new friends with you for a lifetime!

Included in this amazing experience is:

- 3 luxury hotel stays
- 2 domestic flights within Peru
- 6 Breakfasts, 3 lunches & 3 dinners
- Private transfers to all accommodations with the group
- English speaking tour guides throughout the trip
- 4 writing workshops to get your book done with streamlined methods Tara has used over the last 15 years
- 1 hour private consultation with Tara about your manuscript
- Zoom call prior to prep for what to pack and prepare ahead of time
- 3 excursions (Shaman ceremony, Machu Picchu & walking tour) all entrance tickets to and transportation; trains, buses etc.
- Inclusion into Facebook group with other participants to chat and get to know each other ahead of time and ask questions.

What's NOT included:

- Drinks
- Your international flights to and from Peru
- Travel Insurance
- Additional excursions
- Extra meals/ food bought at the hotels
- Bad decisions
- Not actually writing in your manuscript
- You also must have 2 vaccinations to enter the country of Peru and be able to show your vaccination card.
- Your passport must be current and up to date prior to leaving. We will need copies of it to enter all areas of the country.

Contact us to sign up for this amazing journey with like-minded authors in September 2023!! Go to our website and fill out our form https://richterpublishing.com/contact-us/. This is a limited capacity event so we can have a hands on experience for everyone. So we are capping it for a small group of people. Spots will fill up fast!

If you are interested in making your stay longer in Peru, we also have fun add ons after the writing retreat is over. Contact us for more information. We are excited to start this new journey with you!

www.ingramcontent.com/pod-product-compliance
Lightning Source LLC
Chambersburg PA
CBHW060847270326
41934CB00002B/39